D1625791

To Play the Man

The story of Lady Derby and the Siege of
Lathom House, 1643–1645

by Colin Pilkington

Carnegie Publishing, 1991

To Play the Man —
The story of Lady Derby and the
Siege of Lathom House, 1643-45

by Colin Pilkington

This book is dedicated to the memory of my mother
MARJORY MARY PILKINGTON
who gave me the original idea, accompanied me in my research but
unfortunately died before the book could be published

Published by Carnegie Publishing Ltd., Maynard Street, Preston.
Typeset in Caslon Antique and Times by Carnegie Publishing Ltd
Printed by Pindar Graphics (Preston) Ltd.

First edition, August 1991

ISBN 0-948789-60-3

Contents

The Countess of Derby, whose house it was . . . it seems stole the Earl's breeches, when he fled long since into the Isle of Man, and hath in his absence play'd the man at Lathom . . .

The Scottish Dove newspaper, December 1645

On Saturday December 6 after the house was up, there came letters to the Speaker of the Commons' House of the surrender of Lathom House in Lancashire, belonging to the Earl of Derby, which his lady, the Comtesse of Derby, in proving herself of the two a better souldier, hath above these two years kept in opposition to our forces.

. . . The Perfect Diurnall, December 8, 1645

An introduction

N May 1643, after the fall of Warrington to parliamentary forces had signalled the triumph of parliament in the county, Colonel Holland of the Council of the Holy State in Manchester, *de facto* if not *de jure* head of the parliamentarian cause in Lancashire, sent to Lathom House to demand the surrender, and subsequent sequestration, of the House to Parliament. The Earl of Derby, whose principal residence and stronghold Lathom House was, was at that time absent in the Isle of Man about the king's business, and the house was kept in his absence by his wife – the Lady Charlotte de Tremouille. She, backed only by a small garrison, claimed that she could not surrender her husband's house in his absence and without his consent, and rejected Holland's summons out of hand.

The siege began at once, but unofficially, with one man, Alexander Rigby, taking it upon himself to organise a close watch on Lathom House, seeking to prevent supplies and reinforcements from reaching the house, and trying to cut off any communication the garrison might have with royalist forces elsewhere. But, by the February of 1644, Rigby had managed to persuade the Council of the Holy State to endorse his actions as official. From that moment on the siege was continued with increased forces, and with varying degrees of severity, until May 1644 when the house was relieved by a royalist army under the leadership of Prince Rupert, with Lord Derby as his most willing supporter.

That, in brief, is the story of the siege of Lathom House; as much if not more than will be found in any history of the Civil War in England. Yet, of course, there is far more to it than that. It is somewhat ironic that present day ignorance makes such a summary necessary since it is not that long ago since the basic facts concerning the Countess of Derby, and the part she played in the siege at Lathom, were universally known; not only in Lancashire, in which county the siege remains an historical landmark, but throughout the country as a whole. Historical novelists of the nineteenth century, romantic royalists to a man, seized upon the history of the siege and turned it into a part of English folklore by constantly returning to the theme.

Within the Victorian ethos there was, naturally, a good reason for the popularity of the tale. Novelists such as Harrison Ainsworth treated the

Countess of Derby's stance during the siege as a moral fable. She was to be portrayed as a poor, defenceless member of the gentler sex who remained faithful to her husband's cause out of love and loyalty, despite being most cruelly persecuted by heartless men. Only a generation ago schoolchildren such as myself, in the junior schools of the Ormskirk area, were given, as classroom reading, a book that held up Lady Derby as an example of the way steadfast loyalty might well be persecuted, but will eventually triumph; while her parliamentary foes, stigmatised by the pejorative use of the word 'puritan', are condemned as villainous, simply for their lack of chivalry in making war on a woman.

It was not really like that of course; the reality was different, but far more interesting. Even the most rudimentary research into the events of that year will show that, far from being oppressed and terrorised, the Countess, in fact, enjoyed every minute of it; going so far as actually to warn off her husband when he seemed set to intervene, through negotiating a settlement on her behalf. Anyone capable of seeing Lady Charlotte as a poor defenceless woman was totally insensitive to her character and history. As daughter of a powerful Huguenot family in France, the grand-daughter of William the Silent, and related to half the royal families of Europe, Lady Charlotte's upbringing was rooted in power politics, and the religious conflict known as the Thirty Years War. Far from daunted by the challenge sent her, she flourished under adversity, and proved a far more dominant personality than her rather ineffectual husband. As devious as Elizabeth I, as inflexible as Mrs Thatcher and with the physical presence of an Amazon, her part in the siege needs to be completely re-assessed by the historian.

It would be all too easy to over-estimate the historical importance of the siege, and, indeed, it is often done. The events of 1643-1645 have an obvious significance for the inhabitants of South-West Lancashire, since the two sieges at Lathom, and the minor battle near Ormskirk which intervenes, were the only events of any importance to occur in the area in two thousand years of history. Out of a sense of local patriotism it is only natural that people would like to magnify these events, and consider them to be of national importance. I have read several works of local history which speculate along the lines of, 'what a difference it might have made to the royalist cause if . . .' In a recent history of Lathom the words, 'Upon which the fate of England was to depend', were used about the siege of Lathom House. Sadly, the fact is, of course, that the fate of England never did depend upon Lathom House. Indeed, the outcome of the siege was irrelevant even to the course of the war in Lancashire, let alone having any significance whatsoever for the national struggle.

The most striking fact about the official recognition of the siege in 1644 is how totally unnecessary it was. It was a lack of necessity which impressed the more prominent parliamentary leaders such as Thomas Fairfax and Ralph Assheton who withdrew from the siege as soon as it was decently possible, and who distanced themselves from the endeavour thereafter. The fascination of the siege for the historian lies, ironically enough, in its sheer lack of importance. Why was it that, during a period when the respective fortunes of king and parliament were disputed in the Midlands and Yorkshire and the outcome of the war hung in the balance, the parliamentary authorities in Lancashire were ready to commit virtually their entire manpower, at considerable cost to both life and purse, to the capture of a fortified house of no strategic importance?

The need to understand that anomaly is one of the reasons why I think that the story of the siege is still of some importance to the historian, highlighting as it does the contradictions inherent in the Civil War, with ideology on one side and practical soldiering on the other. The siege of Lathom acts as a microcosm of the war as a whole in the character, behaviour and contradictory values of the principal participants, even if in terms of military strategy and tactical advantage it mattered little who was to be the victor at Lathom.

Not that we need be so earnest in seeking a justification for telling the story again. It is now twenty years since I first began to study this story, and I can still find odd facts, snippets of information and sidelines of history that add both to my knowledge and to the general entertainment value of the story. Most interesting however – as I have already hinted – is the way in which the facts as they are revealed insist on overturning one's preconceptions of what happened. I began my researches with my knowledge conditioned by my childhood reading and soon discovered, as stated above, that the orthodox view of Lady Derby's situation is the very reverse of the truth. It is also remarkable how Lady Charlotte's charisma persists over the years. I began my researches determined to be neutral and objective, predisposed if anything to favour the parliamentary view of the conflict – partly because of a sense of fair play which told me that the royalists had had far too good a press for the past three hundred years. Yet, in spite of my intentions, I felt my critical stance vis-a-vis Lady Derby undergo a change from the critical to a grudging respect, and, ultimately, to sheer admiration. Her magic still works.

I should like to express my thanks to those who have encouraged my interest in the siege of Lathom House. To Bill Amos, former editor of *Lancashire Life;* to the BBC in Manchester; and, above all, to the members of the many local history and other societies throughout South-West Lancashire that I have spoken to in the past ten years and who have shown, through their kind applause and interest, that something remains in those distant events that still speaks to the modern imagination. It was those audiences and their oft-repeated complaint that it was impossible to find a recent book about the siege, which inspired me to re-examine my own notes and to embark upon this present work.

Colin Pilkington
Burscough, nr. Ormskirk.

Part One

The background

Chapter One

A brief history of the lordship of Lathom

T may seem rather strange to cast back into history virtually as far as the Dark Ages, when our concern here is with events in the seventeenth century. Yet it is my thesis that the motivations which drew people into following one course of action rather than another during the Civil Wars in Lancashire have their roots in the rise to importance of the lordship of Lathom within Lancashire. How did this small rural backwater come to have such an importance in the affairs of the county? And what passions and secret resentments were engendered over the centuries by the Stanleys in their stewardship of Lathom?

I happen to believe that the course of a developing history is rooted further back in the past than many think, and that events at any one time are determined by a slow accretion of factors over centuries rather than years. For those who find the medieval roots of our society irrelevant to the subject, I recommend that they skip this chapter and go straight to the next. For the rest I think that there may be a real benefit in looking back at the origins of Lathom, and the means whereby it became the virtual capital of Lancashire.

The Domesday Survey

LATHOM as a place, though not yet as a house, makes its first documented appearance in *Domesday Book*, among the entries for Derby Hundred in the lands, attached to Cheshire, but known as 'Between Ribble and Mersey' where, in the time of King Edward –

Uctredus tenebat Latune cum I bereuuicha. Ibi dimidia hide. Silva I leuua longa et dimidia lata. Valebant x solidos et viii denarios. [Uctred held Lathom with one berewick. There is half a hide. Woodland one league long and half a league wide. Valued at ten shillings and eight pence.]

The basis of tax evaluation in the late Anglo-Saxon state was a holding of land sufficient to support one family, which was generally calculated to be approximately 120 acres in extent. The name given to this area of land was generally a 'hide'. In the Danish-speaking North and East, on the other hand, it was known as a 'caracute'. South-west Lancashire, with Danish speakers to the north of the Ribble, and English speakers south of the Mersey, was unique in using both terms simultaneously; a 'caracute' referred to the regular 120 acres, but a 'hide' represented a holding of six caracutes. The manor of Lathom therefore comprised 360 acres of land under cultivation and 720 acres of woodland. There was also the berewick which was a settlement, or township, attached to the manor, and dependent on it, without necessarily forming part of it. It is an educated guess on my part – no more – but I suspect that the berewick attached to the manor of Lathom was the embryonic settlement that would grow, in time, into the town of Ormskirk; which as a settlement is not otherwise mentioned in the Domesday Survey.

At the time *Domesday Book* was drawn up, the area of land between the rivers Ribble and Mersey lay outside the main administrative structure of England. A sort of no-man's land in early Anglo-Saxon times, it had passed, by way of the Viking and Irish-Norse invasions, into forming part of the Danish Kingdom of York. Encroachment on the Danelaw was begun by the son of Alfred, Edward the Elder, and continued by his son, Athelstan. In the process, the lands between Ribble and Mersey were annexed to the Earldom of Mercia; not being granted 'shire' status, but becoming the personal property of the king, divided into six manors, so large as to be known as hundreds, of which the most important was the westernmost – the Hundred of Derby.

When Edward the Confessor died in 1066 the lands of one man, Uctred, held directly from the king, outweighed all others in Derby Hundred, occupying virtually half the hundred's surface area. Uctred held seventeen and a half manors north of the Mersey, and two in Cheshire. The extent of his holdings can be seen on the first of the maps on page eleven. The way in which those holdings are dispersed tells us a

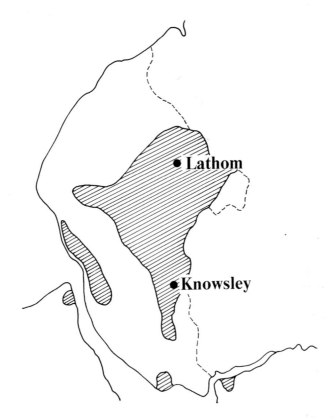

Uctred's holdings in 1066 – the above drawing shows the area covered by the manors held by Uctred in Lancashire and Cheshire in 1066.

great deal. It tells us that Uctred, or rather his ancestor, was granted those particular manors for specific, strategic reasons, on which all the later importance of the holders of Lathom and Knowsley came to depend.

At the time of annexation in the mid-tenth century, two things were a matter of concern for the Mercian English concerning the Danish and Norse occupation of the Lancashire Plain. Firstly, they were afraid of attacks across the Mersey into Cheshire; and secondly, they were concerned about the steady migration from Man or Dublin whereby, having landed their ships on the shallow shore of the Lancashire coast, reinforcements for the Danes of York made their way eastwards by way of the ridgeway formed by the low hills of south-west Lancashire.

A close look at the map will show how Uctred's holdings were designed to contain these two threats, and the form of his lordship must, therefore, have had its roots in Mercian defence policy. The manors fall into three categories. First there is a narrow strip of holdings running from Crosby

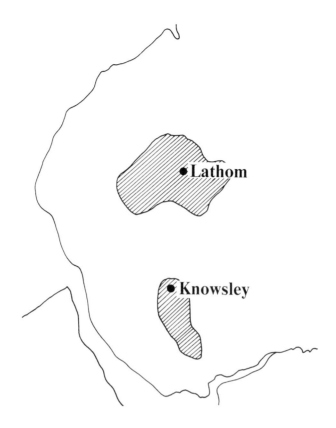

Holdings of the De Lathom family in 1212. The land was held by direct right of thegnage.

to Kirkdale, along the high ground slightly inland from the Mersey estuary, and which obviously formed a first line of defence against any incursions from the sea. Behind that, and across Altcar Moss, lies a large group of manors forming a diamond shape, which exactly covers the two lines of low hills – one running east to west from Ashurst Beacon through Ormskirk to Pinfold Hill in Halsall; the second running north to south from Ormskirk through Knowsley to Allerton and Woolton. Finally, Uctred held three isolated manors, all of which were on the banks of the Mersey, at Wallasey, Speke and Norton. It is surely not a coincidence that these three places were all traditionally, and until fairly recently, the starting points for ferry crossings across the Mersey.

It can therefore be seen that as long ago as 1066, and very probably long before that, the landowner in possession of Lathom filled an important and dominant role in North-West England. Indeed, there must be some significance in the extent to which the holding of Uctred in the eleventh century mirrors the holdings of the Earls of Derby in the seventeenth. It is true that historical geographers such as Hoskins are fond of emphasising the sometimes amazing continuity of land tenure and boundary lines in the English countryside, and here we have an outstanding example. Estates that were in the hands of the Earls of Derby right up to the present century, centred on Lathom and Knowsley, are shown to have been in the hands of one owner even before the Norman Conquest.

It was not only continuity of land tenure, however, but also continuity of family. In 1189 the lord of the manor of Lathom was a Robert Fitzhenry de Lathom. The Norman-French form of his name, and that of his father – Henry de Lathom – may lead one to suppose that the family holding Lathom were part of the Norman-French ascendancy which followed the Conquest. In fact Henry was the first to use the suffix 'de Lathom', and his father was called Siward, whose father in turn was called Dunning. And Dunning takes us back to the immediate post-Conquest period, so that he might well have been the son of Uctred, Henry and Robert may be French enough, but Uctred, Dunning and Siward are all good Anglo-Scandinavian names, commonly found in the family ruling Northumbria during the eleventh century. The family known as the de Lathoms was therefore an English, or Anglo-Danish family, which may well have included Uctred in a continuous line of descent.

It is widely assumed that after 1066 the English aristocracy and land owners were all swept away to be replaced by new Norman-French lords. It was, by no means, the inevitable case. In the immediate aftermath of the Conquest, William tried to maintain the English institutions unaltered, his Norman-French nominees merely being put in where important landowners had fallen or fled at Hastings. That situation, however, changed with the rebellions of 1069 after which William exacted a terrible vengeance, and most of the remaining Anglo-Saxon hierarchy were dispossessed. This was certainly true of the North, where rebellions in York and Chester led William to adopt a burned-earth policy, leading to a devastation, such as had not been seen since the first Viking raids. In Amounderness Hundred, north of Preston, *Domesday Book* records fifty-nine manors existing in 1066, only sixteen of them being inhabited in 1086. In Cheshire, the advance of King William's army on Chester, along the south bank of the Mersey, is recorded by a swathe of manors where a *Domesday Book* entry showing relative prosperity in 1066 is followed by a simple statement for 1086 – 'it is now waste.'

By some means Derby Hundred escaped such destruction. *Domesday* gives a level of tax assessment for 1086 very little changed from 1066. Apparently the thanes of the hundred fought shy of the rebellions, and thereby escaped retribution and confiscation. The lands between Ribble and Mersey were given in their entirety to Roger de Poitou, younger son of Earl Roger de Montgomery. In Derby Hundred, Roger granted land to eight tenants who were of French or Norman descent. But, the extent of the land granted to these eight was less than the total area of tenanted land in the hundred, and it would seem that Uctred – or was it Dunning by now? – was rewarded for his loyalty by being allowed to retain, in thegnage, a strong central block of manors. These manors certainly included Lathom itself, together with Ormskirk; Hurlston, including Scarisbrick; Martin, including Burscough; Aughton, including Bickerstaffe; and Skelmersdale, which took in Dalton. There is no documentary evidence that these lands remained in the hands of Uctred or his family, but there is equally no evidence that they passed into Norman-French hands, while there is a great deal of circumstantial evidence to show that they were held from Roger by an English family.

The Cheshire manors were lost to Uctred, Norton being laid waste. The coastal strip of manors, which included Crosby, was granted to the ancestor of the Molyneux family of Sefton. The southern manors of Uctred's larger holding – those which included Knowsley – were granted, as part of a much wider holding, to William FitzNigel, son of the Constable of Cheshire and Lord of Halton, posts which William later held himself. FitzNigel seemed to take, under Roger de Poitou, much the same position that had been held by Uctred under the English kings – defender of the Mersey crossings and the routes commanding them. FitzNigel's holding was known as the Fee of Widnes, and spread across the whole of South Lancashire. For Uctred this loss of the southern manors, together with a possible wish to keep clear of the troubles north and south of the rivers, probably gave a new importance to the central manors he retained as tenant-in-chief, and this also led to a new importance for the hitherto peripheral manor of Lathom – so that what was the largest manor left in his hands became the most important, the seat of the family, and, ultimately, gave the family its name.

The de Lathom family

THE manor house and main settlement of the manor of Lathom was placed originally on the western edge of the manor, quite close to the boundary with Burscough, and on the present site of Ormskirk Golf Club. The hamlet or settlement that grew up around the manor house was known as Alton, and the house itself as Alton, or Halton Castle. This is just one of a series of coincidences that seem to link Lathom with Halton in Cheshire. The manor of Norton, held by Uctred, was adjacent to Halton and William FitzNigel who was Uctred's successor in so many ways, was also Lord of Halton in succession to the holder in 1066 – Orm.

While Orm, of course, was the name of the otherwise unknown founder of Ormskirk. Such a series of coincidences, culminating in the choice of 'Alton' for a name for the main settlement in Lathom, leads one, inevitably, to the supposition that Uctred came originally from the same family as that which held Halton; one could even postulate the hypothesis that Orm, dispossessed and burnt out of his manor by the Normans, took refuge in Uctred's territory, and hence came to found the church at Ormskirk. Such a suggestion is pure speculation, but it does not conflict with the facts as they are known.

Dunning is a very shadowy figure, whom we know of simply as being the father of Siward. Siward we do know of since he emerges during the reign of Henry I, secure enough in his tenure of Lathom as to be able to grant a caracute of land to Gospatrick of Hindley. Henry FitzSiward, the first to use the family name of 'de Lathom', extended his estates even further. We know, for example, that he acquired the manor of Flixton in the barony of Manchester. It was also probably in his time, if not earlier, that the de Lathoms began to regain some control over their former possessions. In 1212 Richard FitzRobert de Lathom was known to hold the four manors of Roby, Knowsley, Huyton and Tarbuck; the four held as a single knight's fee. Since Richard's father, Robert, in 1189, could grant the rights to the church at Huyton, this sub-tenancy which reunited the manors of Lathom and Knowsley, under a single lord, was presumably an arrangement of long standing.

It is quite clear that, within a century of the Norman Conquest, the de Lathoms had climbed back into that pre-eminence, within Derby Hundred, that had been held by Uctred and his predecessors. In 1189 Robert FitzHenry had wealth and power enough to contemplate the endowment of a religious foundation, establishing the Priory of St. Nicholas on the north western limits of the estate in a bend in the stream which divides Lathom from Burscough. For support of the priory Robert was able to give a land grant of about ten square miles between Burscough, Ormskirk and Lathom as well as the grant of three churches at Ormskirk, Huyton and Flixton. The grandson of that Robert, Robert FitzRichard, achieved the summit of De Lathom success by accepting a knighthood from Henry III and serving two terms as sheriff of the newly-created County of Lancaster between the years of 1249 and 1265.

In 1385, however, having achieved their pre-eminence, the de Lathoms were left without a male heir, and all their lands, power and possessions passed into the hands of the Stanleys on the marriage of Sir John Stanley to the heiress, Isabel de Lathom.

Thomas, Lord Stanley

IT is under the Stanleys that Lathom House developed into the centre of power that it would represent for Lancashire during the fifteenth and sixteenth centuries. That same Sir John Stanley who had married Isabel de Lathom laid the foundation of the family fortune by an adroit transfer of loyalty from Richard II to the usurping Henry IV; for which the Stanleys were duly rewarded by being granted the Lordship of the Isle of Man. But the true architect of the rise in power and prestige for both house and family was Thomas, Lord Stanley. During the anarchic period of the Wars of the Roses, Lord Stanley always managed to be somehow on the victorious side; or, if he were by chance to end on the losing side, was never that deeply implicated so as to lose by it. Originally a Lancastrian, he then transferred successfully to the cause of Edward IV and the Yorkists; only to become embroiled – together with his brother-in-law, Warwick – in the plot to depose Edward and replace Henry VI on the throne. Unlike Warwick, he emerged from the affair, not only with his life and estates intact, but retaining the favour of Edward and being rewarded with high office in the royal household. When the king's brother, Richard, Duke of Gloucester, was lord of the north, he frequently clashed with Lord Thomas over breaches of the peace arising from Stanley's feud with the Harringtons of Hornby Castle. Yet, when Gloucester came to the throne as Richard III, Stanley retained his offices in the royal household despite his having married, as his second wife, Margaret Beaufort, mother of Henry Tudor the Lancastrian pretender.

Paul Murray Kendall, in his biography of Richard III, says of the two Stanleys, Lord Thomas and his brother Sir William, 'Except for the Duke of Norfolk and the Earl of Northumberland, the Stanleys commanded the greatest seigneurial power in England.' That power was gained as a reward for so much duplicity that one wonders at the gullibility of successive kings who placed their trust in the Stanleys, only to have that trust betrayed. Another historical biographer, Charles Ross, in his life of Edward IV, is moved to speak of, 'the shifty Stanley – whose family motto *Sans Changer'* has a splendid historical irony.' The ultimate in Stanley double-dealing came as most people know, at the Battle of Bosworth when, despite solemn promises to mobilise the Lancashire levies in support of the king who had so generously rewarded him, and despite having his heir, Lord Strange, as a hostage in Richard's camp, Lord Thomas remained on the sidelines of the battle until it was clear as to which way it was going, whereupon he gave his full support to the winning side, just in time to greet his wife's son as king.

Henry VII was either less gullible or more suspicious than his Plantagenet predecessors because, despite Stanley's position as husband of the king's mother, Henry refused to trust him with any great office; and was later to execute Lord Thomas's brother, Sir William. Yet, even though he was not entrusted with office by the Tudor, Lord Thomas was amply rewarded in material terms for his part in his stepson's victory. The lands of the many Lancashire families who had loyally supported King Richard were confiscated under act of attainder and transferred into the hands of Lord Stanley. He was also created Earl of Derby, as a further step in his upwardly mobile career, which had now led to such an authority within Lancashire, as to give him virtual vice-regal powers in the county. In spite of the involvement of Sir William Stanley in the Perkin Warbeck affair, a venture that cost him his head, the Stanley family had done very well out of the Wars of the Roses, gaining wealth, power and vast estates. It had also gained them the envious resentment of their former peers, those who had lost their own properties in the aggrandisement of the Stanleys. The fickleness of their behaviour had also lost them the full trust of their monarch. Both these factors were to become prejudices that persisted for more than a century, to the detriment of the seventh earl.

The rapid personal rise of Lord Stanley, later Lord Derby, was shared by a similar enhancement of the new earl's properties; at Lathom House in particular. If Lord Derby was to have near-royal power in Lancashire, he would have to have a near-royal residence to match. Extensive alterations to the house and additional building works were undertaken in the period following Bosworth in 1485; increasingly so after Derby learned that his stepson, the king, was to visit Lathom in 1496. Such extensive work must, it seems, have produced an imposing result, because it is said that the king was so impressed by Lathom House that he gave instructions to his architects that they should take the house for their model in the design of the palace at Richmond that was then under construction.

The Tudor Period – embellishments

SUCH building works as had been undertaken during the fifteenth century – and they had been considerable – had had a dual purpose that was as much military as domestic, producing a fortress as well as a home. During the sixteenth century the Stanleys turned to a more peaceful architecture and the enhancement of their environment through the development of their estate.

The first addition to the estate was planned by the first earl, but it only reached fruition under his son. This was a chantry chapel linked to a charitable foundation in which masses could be said for the soul of the founder. Permission for this was granted by the Bishop of Lichfield, in

1509, in the time of the second earl. An elegant little chapel was built together with eight adjoining almshouses, dedicated to St. John the Divine, and consecrated in a service conducted by the Bishop of Sodor and Man.

This chapel is the only building erected prior to the siege that has survived to the present day. Records show that worship was continuous at the chapel right up to the time of the siege, and throughout the troubled period that followed. It must be emphasised that this was not intended to be the chapel for the house; there was a chapel within the walls for the family and their immediate attendants. The Chapel of St. John served as a chantry until the Reformation; and as a chapel for tenants on the estate after that.

About the same time work began on the rehabilitation of Halton Castle, and whatever was left of the original manor house was replaced by a house built in a more up-to-date, domestic style. The land previously attached to Halton Castle was now enclosed and turned into a deer park, both house and deer-park being known as New Park. The earls of the sixteenth century seemed to favour their new home at New Park. Certainly, in the time of Elizabeth I, the fourth earl spent much of his time there. From existing records we know that he entertained lavishly there, and much of his correspondence as Lord Lieutenant of the county was written from 'my howse at Newparke'.

By the end of the sixteenth century, and the start of the seventeenth, the prestigious position of the Earls of Derby, and of Lathom House, were firmly established. His own position in Lancashire pre-eminent, the earl lived in a house of such grandeur that a king could model his palace upon it. Earl of Derby and Lord of Man, Lord-Lieutenant of Lancashire and the virtual feudal overlord of the Hundred of West Derby; the Stanley of his day could live in his house at Knowsley, hold court at Lathom, or receive visitors at New Park, in near regal splendour. 'It was the custom in the county then,' wrote a contemporary chronicler, 'when pledging their loyal toast, to pledge 'The Earl of Derby and the King', and by thus placing the name of their earl before that of their monarch, showed by their harmless treason their devotion to the Earl of Derby.'

Such was the confidence of the Stanleys in their position within the county, that they could not really envisage a time when that same sense of their own importance would militate against them. Nor could anyone dream of a time when the house at Lathom would itself become a symbol; so that the disaffected would not only seek the destruction of the House of Stanley in the metaphoric sense of stripping the Earls of Derby of every last vestige of power, but in the strictly literal sense of demolishing Lathom House itself. Yet, unthinkable though it may have been, there were those who, during the Civil War, made the destruction of the House the motivation that, above all else, guided their actions and policy.

Chapter Two

The House – its nature, location and surroundings

n light of the importance that the house itself would assume in the story of the siege, it is a sad irony that only the vaguest of descriptions exists to tell us what the house actually looked like. The demolition which followed the final capitulation, was, perhaps, not as complete as had been foreseen in parliament's instruction to reduce the house, 'as if it had never been.' There is some evidence that a later earl lived among the ruins of the old house for a time. Yet, what parliament had left undone, the builders and developers of the following century completed. By the time artists came to understand that houses might be a fit subject to be immortalised by their art, not a stone stood above ground to show even where the house had stood, let alone what it had looked like.

A picture does exist. This is an engraving which originally appeared in Seacome's *Historical Account of the House of Stanley,* which was published originally in the late-eighteenth century. It is carefully stated, however, that the drawing is 'reconstructed from existing documents'. In other words, this is an artist's impression, executed more than a century after the house ceased to be. Indeed, it is very probable that the 'existing documents' mentioned appear in the self same work by Seacome, in the form of the one written description we do possess, purporting to be a brief account written by Samuel Rutter, chaplain to Lady Charlotte at the time of the siege. This short passage by Rutter, as included by Seacome in his work, describes the house as it was during the siege and therefore concentrates rather on the defensive fortifications, instead of telling us much about the lay-out of the house itself. The passage is also rather on the hard side for the modern reader to understand; as seventeenth-century syntax, style, vocabulary and usage are very different to the language of today.

According to Seacome, repeating the description given by Rutter, the

An artist's impression of how Lathom House might have looked, before the siege. The engraving is based on contemporary descriptions such as Samuel Rutter's, and was used to illustrate Seacome's Account of the House of Stanley, *first published in the 1790s.*

The site of both old and later Lathom Houses, seen from the roadway close to Lathom Park Chapel. The landscape is fairly featureless but it can be seen that the ground rises to form a plateau from a point just right of the remaining wing of the later house, to the far right of the picture where the ground starts to slope away again. [Photo author.]

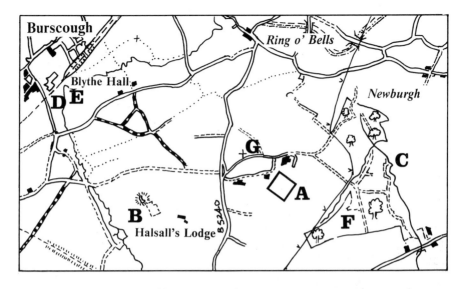

Lathom House and its surroundings

A map showing Lathom House and its environs in a period before the construction of Pilkington's Glass Research Laboratories. Enlarged to a scale of 2 inches to the mile and showing sites of places mentioned in the text.

A – Probable site Lathom House pre-1645.
B – Known site of New Park House.
C – Location 'Cromwell's Stone' in Tawd Valley, probable site parliamentarian camp.
D – Site of Burscough Priory.

E – Location of Burscough Mill.
F – Brook, tributary of the Tawd, possibly that named as Golforden in *The Journal Of the Siege*. Earthworks, probably siege-works.
G – Lathom Park Chapel

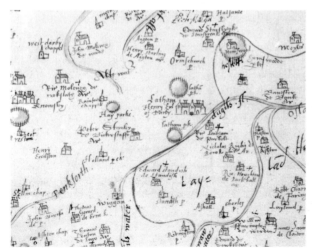

A section of Burghley's map of Lancashire of the 1570s. It was drawn to show Elizabeth I's minister, Lord Burghley, the seats of the Roman Catholic gentlemen of Lancashire.

In the centre of the section can be seen an early representation of Lathom House and park.

West is at the top of the picture.
[British Museum.]

house at Lathom –

Standing on a flat moorish, springy and spumous ground, was at the time of the siege encompassed with a strong wall, of two yards thick; upon the wall were nine towers, flanking each other, and in every tower were six pieces of ordnance that played three one way and three the other.

Without the wall, was a moat, eight yards wide, and two yards deep; upon the brink of the moat, between the wall and the graff, was a strong row of palisadoes, and, to add to these securities, there was a high tower called the Eagle Tower, in the midst of the house, surrounding all the rest; and the gatehouse was also a strong and high building with a strong tower on each side of it; and in the entrance to the first court, upon the top of these towers, were placed the best and choicest marksmen.

Apart from recognising that there is a tendency to use semi-colons in places where we would put a full stop, it is perhaps necessary to clarify the meaning of this passage by examining the sense of an archaic word, no longer used, and one obsolete usage of a word still in current use. First the word 'graff', which comes from the same root as the Dutch 'gracht', or 'canal', and which is defined by the OED as, 'a trench serving as a fortification; a foss, a moat.' The second point refers to the use of 'surrounding' in the passage which speaks of the Eagle Tower, 'surrounding all the rest'. It has to be realised that the original meaning of 'surrounding' was, literally, 'flooding over', and was used in the sense of 'overlooking' or 'over-topping'. The passage is merely saying, therefore, that the Eagle Tower was higher than all the other towers in the house.

The bare description given above is obviously in need of fleshing out from other sources. No other description exists, as such, but occasional references in other works can add details that give more substance to our impression of what the house was like. The most important of these other works is, in fact, the source for most of our knowledge concerning events during the siege. This is a journal kept by a member of the garrison, and takes the form of a daily diary of events. The diary is, of course, more concerned with what was happening than with describing the house, but the mere fact of saying what was happening in the house tells us something of what the house was like.

Take, for example, the walls which Rutter described as being a strong wall of two yards thick, and merely adds the fact of there being an outer fence of timber palisades between the stone wall and the moat. The diary gives us the additional information that the walls were thirty feet high, as well as six feet thick, and that, as well as the outer timber fence, a bank of turves helped to reinforce the inner side of the walls; no doubt fulfilling the same role in the siege as sandbags served in later wars.

In all accounts a great emphasis is placed on the main gateway, which must have been an imposing structure designed to impress the visitor. It seems to have been a barbican, rather than a simple gate, with a gate set into an arch beneath a gatehouse and flanked by two towers that were much higher than the walls. One reading of the words, 'and in the entrance to the first court' could well imply that this barbican was four-sided, with a tower at each corner, linking the outer world with the first courtyard of the house. Since there is no mention of a bridge or drawbridge, we can assume that the gatehouse projected across and beyond the moat.

One point that is clear in the journal, though not in the description quoted by Seacome, is that there was more than one gateway to the house. Several accounts of attacks made by the garrison on the besiegers mention them making twin-headed attacks, with one party leaving by the main gate while a second exits by way of a sally-port. One later passage actually speaks of a postern tower and gate, situated on the north-eastern side of the house directly opposite the main gate; this postern tower being said to project beyond the moat so as to allow egress and access without there being a bridge across the ditch.

There is no doubt, whatsoever, that the house within the walls was large and extensive. If one views the site, from about a mile to the north, so that the lie of the land stands out against the horizon, the raised ridge on which the house stood can be seen quite clearly forming a plateau-like mound quite three hundred yards in length from front to back. Making due allowance for the nine towers, and for a reasonable stretch of wall between each tower, we must be talking of an area within the wall of at least five acres, and probably more. At one time or another during the siege, a garrison of three hundred; the countess with her family and household; a number of royalist refugees; servants; and an indefinite number of dependents such as officer's wives; were all housed within the walls. The house had to be large.

In the journal, and elsewhere, a somewhat ambiguous form of wording has the effect of saying that the nine towers on the walls were mirrored by a further nine towers within the house itself. Two of these are named, one being the Eagle Tower – bigger and taller than the rest – and the other being the Chapel Tower. The latter must also have contained a belfry, as the journal records that the chapel bell was rung four times every day on each day of the siege. It has been assumed that the walls and towers of the house were built of stone, but this need not have been the case. The house was renovated in a period when brick was coming into favour for the construction of the grander and more pretentious of buildings; and it is certainly true that the clay soils of south-west Lancashire would be more likely to provide the raw material for bricks than building stone. It is probably the case that brick was partially used, although stone is still more likely to have been used for the fortifications and the large towers such as the Eagle Tower.

The range of buildings which linked the towers, and which formed the domestic accommodation for the house, had a lower storey of stone or brick, but upper storeys of timber-framed lath and plaster construction.

This can be inferred from the period late in the siege, when the besiegers began to bombard the house with explosive grenades fired from a mortar. One soldier, we are told, had a narrow escape while sleeping in an upper room when a piece of shrapnel from a fragmenting grenade passed right through the room in which he lay, coming in through one wall and leaving through the other. During the mortar bombardments there was a mutiny on the part of soldiers in the garrison who refused to sleep in the upper rooms, which had 'walls of clay', unless their officers would share in their dangerous accommodation. These incidents, and the general fear that was engendered by the mortar, do suggest very strongly that much of the house was fairly fragile in its construction. And it has to be said that a combination of stone, brick and half-timbering, was not uncommon in houses built during the fourteenth and fifteenth centuries when most of Lathom House was constructed.

The buildings of which the house was made up, were arranged in a series of courtyards and quadrangles. We know of at least three such courtyards from one source or another – there was the first court mentioned as being within the gate; the inner or central courtyard which gave access to the Eagle Tower; and there was a disused court in the old part of the house within which a mortar grenade exploded, in the latter part of the siege.

The impression we gain from these various sources is of a house that grew in size over the years by adding another building, or another wing, to the existing buildings, until the space within the walls had become a rabbit-warren of interlocking buildings. Crammed together were impressive public rooms such as the Banqueting Hall and the Great Hall; domestic apartments and living-quarters for family, garrison and servants; any number of out-buildings, stables, coach-houses, sheds and huts, all serving a variety of purposes. The over-riding impression is of a house that once was very grand, but is now past its best. No matter how prestigious it may have been in the past as the principal house of the Earls of Derby, it had now become just a little old-fashioned, uncomfortable and not very popular. The seventh earl's grandfather had preferred to live at New Park, his father had moved to Bidston-on-the-Wirral as soon as possible, while both James Stanley and Lady Charlotte seemed to have preferred Knowsley or the Isle of Man to Lathom.

Our assumptions as to the look and nature of Lathom House have to be founded on speculation. Apart from the fact that all above-ground traces of the house have long since disappeared, there is not free access to the site, and no archaeological exploration has been permitted since the demolition of the later house in 1920. New Park House on the other hand, has been extensively investigated, and the results of excavation there can be read in The Park, Moat and House at New Park, Lathom, a paper by Steane and Kelsall, published in Vol. 114 of the *Transactions of the Historical Society of Lancashire and Cheshire, 1962* (pp.73-98).

The house at New Park was much smaller than Lathom House itself, but was still a substantial property of sixteenth-century construction, complete with castellations, and set within a moat. Traces of the moat still survive, and can be seen marked on ordnance survey maps of the area, situated in the centre of Ormskirk Golf Club's course. Attached to the house was a large, brick-walled garden, a substantial dove-cote, the steward's house and the home farm. New Park may not have had the grandeur of the big house in Lathom Park, but it was a not insubstantial, cosy and prosperous estate.

The Location of the House

EVEN today very little obtrudes upon the area within which the siege was enacted, with the somewhat overwhelming exception of Pilkington's Glass Research Laboratories. Yet even that bulky structure can assist us in recreating the past in that the way in which the Glass Laboratories seem to catch the eye from no matter where one looks in the area, reminds us of the way in which the bulk of Lathom House must have dominated the view of everyone living in the district. We are told that when Henry VII visited Lord Stanley at Lathom, the earl took his stepson onto the leads of the Eagle Tower in order to show him the vast spread of countryside visible from that height. And it obviously follows that the same wide stretch of countryside that could be seen from the house could also see the house in their turn; its brooding presence must always have been there in the consciousness of people living in the Ormskirk district. In the debate over the location of the house, that need for the house to dominate the area must be borne in mind. The house must have been set upon some eminence, and not hidden away in some wooded dell.

Apart from the recent growth of the glass laboratories, there has been some extension of the land under cultivation, and a few houses have been built along Hall and Spa Lanes. In later years, the land in the vicinity of the later house was tamed into the formation of the home park to the house, and was therefore tamed from the natural state that must have existed at the time of the siege. Also in the intervening centuries some attempts at commercialisation intruded, first with the exploitation of the mineral water spring that gives Spa Lane its name, and then with the coal-mines, drift and shaft, which extended into the park from Skelmersdale. Such forerunners of industrialism have long since failed, and their works disappeared. The extension of cultivation, the making of parkland, even the exploitation of mineral resources, all these have changed the surface appearance of the land, but it has not been built up, and the bare bones of the landscape remain open to the gaze, and the logistics of the siege can still be plotted on the ground today. It means that in attempting to locate the seventeenth-century house we can compare contemporary accounts with the topography of today and know that the two can be reconciled.

The area, as a whole, can best be seen from the B5240 which, as Hall Lane, runs from north to south along the division between Lathom Park and New Park. On the right, as one proceeds northwards along Hall Lane, one's gaze tends to be caught and dominated by the research laboratories, and the view is partly obscured by walls and trees. Nevertheless, it is possible to pick out certain salient features. Furthest south is the highest land in the vicinity of the site – a wooded knoll behind the Plough public house, on which stands a farmhouse. From this high point the ground slopes downwards towards the north-east, levelling out after two or three hundred yards, before rising again past the glass research laboratories to end in a long and almost flat summit, at the northern end of which can be seen the remaining wing of the later Lathom House.

From a halfway point along Hall Lane it is possible to follow the signpost for Lathom Park Chapel, and to enter the park along a private road as far as the chapel. It is from this road that the best unobstructed views of the site are possible, and one is able to confirm that there is a long, rounded plateau to the right of the remaining wing of the later house, up to which the land slopes from all directions. In my opinion, this plateau is without doubt the site of the original house.

Up until a century ago no one would have questioned that last statement, it being taken for granted that the later Lathom House occupied the same site as the earlier. In 1889 a Rev. T. Buxton delivered a lecture in Southport which was intended to prove conclusively that this was the case. Most of his argument rested on discoveries made when extensive repairs were made to the fabric of the house in the 1850s and 1860s. Among other things, alterations to the structure revealed a number of skeletons, stonework from a stained glass window, stones engraved with the Derby crest and, most importantly of all, the discovery that the entire southern front of the later house '. . . is built up to and abuts upon an ancient wall of rubble stone.' The existence of this wall was further confirmed when the main wing was demolished in 1920. To these discoveries Buxton added the continual discovery of musket balls and other detritus of war all over the fields surrounding the site.

Unfortunately in a way, Buxton went on to supplement these fairly strong arguments with suppositions based on features within the Park, the validity of which was far more questionable. Buxton claimed, for example, that the long depression known locally as 'Cromwell's Trench' was part of the besiegers' works. He also equated the ha-ha, a concealed wall which surrounded the formal gardens, with the moat of the old house. Both identifications are dubious to say the least, and, in questioning them, the whole of Buxton's more solid evidence is cast into doubt. The evidence produced by Buxton and confirmed by later discoveries, seems to suggest that the two houses were contiguous in that the southernmost walls of the later house touched, or overlaid, the northernmost walls of the original. Disregarding Buxton's more suspect claims regarding the trench and ha-ha, there are physical remains which suggest that the Lathom House of Civil War times occupied most of the space that now exists between the remaining wing of the later Lathom House to the north and Pilkington Laboratories to the south.

Once Buxton's theories were questioned, however, even in part, there were bound to be those who dismissed the whole thesis and began to look for an alternative location for Lathom House elsewhere. And there is an alternative site close to hand in the valley of the little stream known as the Spa or Slate Brook, some half mile to the south-east of the later house. Here, in a low-lying, wooded area known as Spa Roughs, there are indubitably extensive earthworks which can be interpreted as a rectangular moat and rampart enclosing an area about two hundred yards square. The site in Spa Roughs has acquired many adherents over the years, and it has to be said that the physical evidence for the Spa Roughs site is every bit as strong as that put forward by Buxton for what we might call the 'traditional' site. And, if we give equal weight to the physical evidence, the final verdict as to the location of the house must rest on an interpretation of the description given in Seacome's book and, unfortunately, the ambiguities in that account can still leave two opposing viewpoints equally convinced that they are right.

The first person I know of to challenge received opinion as to the House's location was E. Broxap in his *The Great Civil War in Lancashire,* published by Manchester University Press in 1905. The starting point of his criticism was to say that the ha-ha, which Buxton claimed was the moat, was in fact a dry ditch which could never have held water. And, since there was no other remaining evidence of a moat in the vicinity of the later house, then the older house must have been located elsewhere. The main thrust of his argument is, however, based on a reading of Seacome's description and of certain references in the journal of the siege, all of which according to Broxap located the house in a much hillier and more wooded environment than the open ground around the later house. As a result he suggested that an alternative site should be looked for in the valley of the Tawd.

In 1979, Broxap's view was taken up enthusiastically, and with considerable initiative, by a group of sixth form girls from Holly Lodge School in Liverpool, helped by staff from the Liverpool Institute of Higher Education. As a research project the girls carried out a topographical survey of the earthworks in Spa Roughs and concluded that these were, without doubt, the remains of the moat and fortifications of the older Lathom House. Their findings have since been checked and endorsed by the Civil War historian, Mike Lawson, who goes one step further in claiming to have located the site of the Eagle Tower in Spa Roughs.

Their arguments are very persuasive, and the Holly Lodge exercise was carried out with commendable expertise. Nevertheless, I do believe that simple logic and the remains discovered on the site of the later house lead to the conclusion that the area to the immediate south of the eighteenth-century house is the most likely site of its predecessor. Obviously, I also believe that Seacome's description and the other contemporary accounts support my viewpoint, and that adherents of the Spa Roughs school of thought are basing their similar claims on misinterpretations. So I should like to look again at that description to show where the two conflicting interpretations arise.

As already stated, Seacome's description begins '. . . standing upon a flat, moorish, springy and spumous ground.' Those seeking to place the house in Spa Roughs have taken the words 'springy' and 'spumous' to mean that the ground was wet and marshy. Indeed the Holly Lodge report states with some satisfaction '. . . the presence of ponds and streams is also significant and the moist and spongy nature of the ground is noticeable.' I, on the other hand, would say that the significant word is 'moorish'. In other words the house was set in moorland, and the 'springy, spumous' nature refers to the wiry, mat-like grass and vegetation one gets on a moor. Apart from which I would suggest that a building which had stone walls thirty feet high and six feet thick, as well as numerous stone towers, would need rather more substantial foundations than boggy, water-logged semi-marshland.

The Holly Lodge assessment also makes play of the fact that medieval moats are usually sited in low-lying areas for the retention of water. Yet all accounts of the siege are agreed that one of the main works of the besiegers was a trench '2 yards wide and 3 deepe, for the fall of water' designed as a 'deep sluice to letten out the water in the Mote.'

Such a drain would only work if it approached the moat from a lower level; it would hardly drain away the water if the moat were already low-lying. Which brings us back to Seacome's description and the question as to whether its ambiguous wording means that the house was set up high or within a depression.

The relevant section reads:

before the house, to the south and south-west, there is a rising ground so near as to overlook the top of it, which falls so quick that nothing planted against it on those sides can touch it, further than the front walls. And on the north and east sides there is another rising ground, even to the edge of the moat, and then falls away so quick that you can scarce, at the distance of a carbine shot, see the house over the height . . . and let us observe, by the way, that the uncommon situation of it may be compared to the palm of a man's hand, flat in the middle and covered with a rising ground about it.

The wording is obscure to the modern eye and open to a variety of interpretations. And the phrase most open to misinterpretation is 'rising ground'. Both Broxap and the Holly Lodge team take the phrase to mean that the ground rises steadily in all directions from the house so that the house, which they believe was low-lying, was at the bottom of a hollow. Indeed, the Holly Lodge report states categorically about the Spa Roughs site, 'the land beyond the Slate Brook is rising steadily and overlooks the platform where the house would have stood.' Yet any such interpretation is founded on a partial reading and ignores the repetition of the words 'falls away so quick'. It is clear from Seacome's description that there was indeed an up-slope on the far side of the moat from the house that might almost have reached the height of the walls, but that, almost immediately, the land falls away again in a down-slope. Note that on the north and east – the direction that in Spa Roughs would be represented by the 'land beyond the Slate Brook' – the ground slopes away so steeply that an observer some two hundred yards away can hardly see the upper part of the house over the height of the intervening slope.

The most decisive argument for stating that the house was set above the besiegers rather than below them, comes in the difficulty they found in deploying their cannon. The critical passage in the description quoted above is the one that states, 'which falls away so quick that nothing planted against it on those sides can touch it.' The world 'plant', in this, means to 'establish an artillery battery', according to the O.E.D., and it reminds us that the besiegers suffered the recurring problem throughout the siege of being unable to depress their cannon sufficiently so as to bring them to bear on the vulnerable lower sections of the walls. At one time or another cannon-shot demolished pinnacles on the towers, removed sections from the upper parapet of the walls, and hit the height of the Eagle Tower on many occasions. Yet only once, and that probably by a fluke, did the besiegers' cannon manage to strike the wooden gates of the house. At the north-eastern postern it is stated that the cannon could not be depressed to cover the gate, and that the garrison could advance on the cannon from the house under the line of fire. All of which means that the cannon were mounted on an up-slope because the ground fell away from the house on all sides, and that the lower sections of the house walls were hidden from the besiegers by the ground in-between.

The final part of Seacome's description comparing the site with the palm of a man's hand means that the house was set within a depression, but it was a shallow, saucer-like depression. The rising ground around it was little more than an earth rampart beyond the moat. It is worth remembering that the word 'moat' could mean both the ditch and the embankment formed from the earth taken in digging the ditch, and it is probably this embankment that is meant by the 'rising ground even to the edge of the moat'. All of which could refer to the Spa Roughs site where the remains do show clear indications of a ditch and bank construction, if it were not for the very clear statements that the ground falls away again on all sides, which means that we must look for this large, saucer-like depression, surrounded by an earth embankment, as being set within a plateau at the summit of an eminence if not a hill. And the well-defined plateau between the site of the later house and the glass laboratories, possesses all the requisite features.

It could well be said by the proponents of the Spa Roughs alternative that this does not explain the lack of traces of house or moat on the above-mentioned plateau. Yet a look at a large-scale nineteenth-century map will show that a large circular area to the south of the later house, pretty well filling that plateau, was set out as a series of walks and formal gardens; in other words it had been extensively landscaped after the building of the later house in 1734, and it can be assumed that any traces which remained were destroyed or buried in that process.

There is an obvious alternative explanation for the fortified earthworks in Spa Roughs. According to Peter Draper's *History of the House of Stanley*, the main parliamentary camp was situated in the Tawd Valley, around the spot where the so-called Cromwell Stone was located and where it is marked on the Ordnance Survey map. According to Draper, the besiegers made their way between their camp and their forward positions along the stream which Draper calls the Golforden, but which is identified as the Slate or Spa Brook. That their forward position, from which their trenches and siege-works radiated, was located in a valley or hollow we know from the wording in the siege journal, 'enemy's nightworks which were begun about a musket-shot from the house in a stooping declining ground that their pioneers by the nature of the place might be secured from our ordnance on the towers.' It is, therefore, suggested that the most logical explanation for the earth-works on the banks of the Slate Brook is that they formed the fortified forward position of the besieging forces during the siege.

A final word about the 'Cromwell Stone' which stands in the entrance to Lathom Park Chapel, where it has finally been moved from its original place on the banks of the Tawd opposite that stream's confluence with the Slate Brook. Not that the stone has anything to do with Cromwell of course; it is merely an English custom to credit Oliver Cromwell personally with everything done by parliamentary forces during the Civil Wars. It is claimed that the boulder, which has a number of clearly defined holes in its surface, was used as a mould for musket balls and other lead shot. That is doubtful, and the holes are very probably much older than seventeenth-century, but the folklore connection which gives the stone its name obviously links it with the siege and, as stated above, it probably marks the site of the parliamentary camp.

Chapter Three

For King and Parliament – some of those involved

James Stanley, 7th Earl of Derby

ORD Derby plays a remarkably small part in the events of the siege, and yet his very person, character, and even existence, are so central to the motivations of the besiegers that he is, himself, the *sine qua non* of the entire action.

Born in 1606, he was thirty-six years of age when the siege began in 1643. A tall man, he was said to have a commanding presence. He wore a moustache but not a beard; while his hair was worn long, but straight, without the extravagances of cavalier fashion. As to his personality, there is a conflict between those who revered him and those, equally as many, who hated him. Like his monarch, the manner of his death has sanctified his memory, and the title of 'Martyr Earl' awarded him, has made speaking ill of him a heinous offence, akin to blasphemy, in the eyes of later generations.

If one accepts the view of J. J. Bagley, as the admiring biographer of James Stanley, he was brave, cautious, steadfast and loyal. He was deeply devout and an intellectually religious man, disliking intensely the frivolous pursuits of the royal court. He shunned London and court circles; delighting instead in domestic happiness at home with his family, either in Lancashire or the Isle of Man. Opposed to that sympathetic viewpoint we have the opinion, expressed by C. V. Wedgwood, that the seventh earl was 'narrow-minded, vain and silly; his warfare being brutal because he felt that rebellion in Lancashire was a personal affront to the House of Stanley'.

My own opinion is that it is not impossible for both estimates of his character to be correct, in that what are vices to one perspective can be virtues to another; so that 'steadfast' can equate with 'stubborn', 'cautious' with 'indecisive', and 'deeply religious' with 'narrow-minded'. I do doubt, however, Stanley's intelligence and effectiveness. His military campaigns were not noticeably successful, and the way in which the loss of his army at Whalley in 1643 was duplicated, almost exactly, in the way he lost another army at Wigan in 1651, tempts one to paraphrase the words of Lady Bracknell and say that to lose one army might 'be regarded as a misfortune; to lose both looks like carelessness.'

James only became Lord Derby in September 1642, on the death of his father but, because of the eccentricity of the sixth earl, he had carried out the duties associated with the earldom for quite some time. William Stanley, the sixth earl, had inherited the title unexpectedly on the death of his elder brother Ferdinando, the fifth earl, in 1596. William was not only out of the country at the time, but was believed to be dead. On his 'return from the dead' as it were, in 1597, it was to find that the Stanley wealth and estates had been divided between Ferdinando's three daughters. The ensuing law suits lasted until 1604, and left the Stanley estate other than that attached to the earldom much reduced.

Whether because of disenchantment as a result of these troubles, or because of a naturally retiring disposition, the sixth earl did not enjoy his office. As soon as his son James had achieved his majority, in 1627, he began to surrender the estates and duties of the earldom to his son so that, ultimately, he could retire to his house at Bidston on the Wirral and leave James Stanley, then Lord Strange, in full possession of Lathom, the Isle of Man, Knowsley and the Lord Lieutenancy of Lancashire.

James Stanley married at the age of twenty, although his bride was a few years older than he. The Lady Charlotte de Tremouille was regarded as a splendid match for the young man, and their wedding at The Hague was an occasion graced by the royalty and aristocracy of half of Europe. It might have been expected that Lord Strange would play a leading role in English political life, but, partly because of the burdens placed upon him by his father, partly because of his dislike for court life, but also, possibly, as a result of antipathy between his French Protestant wife and the French Catholic queen, the married couple spent most of their time on their estates in Lancashire, immersed in local rather than national affairs.

Charles I exhibited an almost pathological distrust of the Stanleys, despite the instinctive loyalty shown by the earl for his king. But then it sometimes seemed that Charles distrusted most of his more devoted followers, his mistreatment of Montrose and Prince Rupert probably costing him even more than his mishandling of Derby. The reasons for the king's distrust are rooted deep in his own complex character, but it is certain that part of that distrust was based on the behaviour of Thomas, the first Earl of Derby, at Bosworth. The battle might have been nearly two hundred years in the past, but to Charles's mind it proved that the Stanleys were not to be trusted on the battlefield. He was also said to be afraid that Stanley had aspirations to royalty as was shown by his marriage to a lady with so many royal connections, and he genuinely believed that Lord Derby was merely waiting for the right moment before transforming the Lordship of Man, which was after all held independently of the English crown, into the Kingdom of Man.

Lady Charlotte de Tremouille, Countess of Derby

IF Lord Derby, despite his importance, is merely peripheral, and no more than a catalyst as far as the action of the siege is concerned, Lady Derby holds centre stage throughout, and quite easily dominates it.

She was born in 1599 according to one account, in 1601 according to another; and was, therefore, between forty-two and forty-four years of age at the time of the siege. In appearance she was hardly beautiful, but was without doubt striking, being described as, 'a well-built, almost fleshy woman, having large eyes, heavy eyebrows and a prominent nose.' In character the same source described her as, 'at once haughty and humble. She was pious and would, out of pride, stubbornly hold to a cause which she regarded as her duty . . . and would look with contempt upon anyone who offended her code.' The evidence of the siege shows that she had a considerable intelligence, a shrewd grasp of the principles of negotiation, together with the ability to use histrionics and self-dramatisation as a means to getting her own way. A skilled propagandist, she was also a far more effective tactician than her husband.

Her father was Claude de Tremouille, Duc de Thouars, a leader of the French Huguenots in the Wars of Religion. Her mother, another Charlotte, was the third daughter of William of Orange, nicknamed 'The Silent', the leader of the Protestant Netherlands in their revolt against Spanish rule and founder of the Dutch royal house of Orange-Nassau. She was also the niece of Frederick, the Elector-Palatine, and so cousin of Prince Rupert.

The marriage with James Stanley was a dynastic alliance, an arranged marriage of convenience, the bridegroom five years younger than the bride. And yet no-one could doubt that the marriage was successful with bonds of real affection forged between the pair. Lady Charlotte bore her husband nine children of whom she was obviously very fond. Although most of the children were sent away to a place of safety during the Civil War, two of her younger daughters, Mary and Catherine, were with her at Lathom House throughout the siege.

Samuel Rutter D.D.

SELDOM obtrusive, yet nevertheless omnipresent, as *eminence grise* to her ladyship, was Samuel Rutter, chaplain, friend and adviser to the earl and countess. We do not know his exact date of birth but, since he went up to Oxford in 1623, he can be regarded as an exact or near contemporary of James Stanley.

In appearance he was portly, and looked like the cleric he was, with a liking for dark-coloured clothing and a contemplative manner. He came from the family which owned the mill in Burscough. Within the context of the seventeenth-century village economy, this made the Rutter family into persons of some standing and wealth. That did not, however, put them in anything like the social position of the Stanley family, and the most the young Rutter could have aspired to would have been a grammar school education, followed by a career in the family business. Instead, some talent in the young man must have recommended him, because he was taken up as a protégé by the Stanleys, who sponsored and paid for his education both at Westminster School and Christ Church, Oxford.

His ordination must have coincided with Lord James and Lady Charlotte assuming the responsibilities of the sixth earl. Rutter was appointed as personal chaplain to the then Lord and Lady Strange, later becoming tutor to their first-born son. During the siege he was in constant attendance upon Lady Charlotte, holding four services a day in the chapel throughout the time when the house was invested. At one particular moment he was to play a very important role in the game of intelligence and disinformation that characterised the opening nego-tiating period of the siege; an intervention which was to have a crucial and decisive effect on the course and conduct of the siege.

William Farrington of Worden

AS well as Rutter, Lady Charlotte's principal adviser in the absence of her husband was William Farrington of Worden Hall in Leyland. He was a prominent figure in the county, having been Sheriff of Lancashire in 1636, and one of King Charles's Commissioners of Array. Because of his status, both in the county and in the royalist ranks, he was an early target for the parliamentary sequestrators, and he had lost his house and lands as a result of his refusal to compound with the parliamentary commissioners. He was present in Lathom House as a refugee and pensioner.

Others in the Garrison

THE men who made up the garrison of the House during the siege fall into one of three categories. There were mercenaries hired by Lord Derby as a professional garrison; there were refugees from parliamentary action like Farrington of Worden; and there were officers and men who had served with Derby, and who were left behind by him during his visit of late May, 1643, before his departure for the Isle of Man.

Most notable of the first category was Captain William Farmer, a Scot and professional soldier who had – like so many of the more skilled soldiers on both sides – learned his trade in the Low Countries during the Thirty Years War. He commanded the garrison under Lady Charlotte, and held the title of 'Major of the House'.

There were six named captains about whom little more is known, apart from their names and places of origin. Henry Ogle of Whiston, Edward Chisnall – or Chisenhale – of Chorley, Edward Rawstorne of New Hall near Preston, Molyneux-Ratcliffe of Ordsall and Richard Foxe of Prestwich. The majority of these had served with Derby; Chisnall, Ratcliffe and Rawstorne having, for example, been with Derby at the taking of Preston in March 1643. Two of them were later promoted colonel; Rawstorne became governor of Lathom House and commanded during the second siege; while Chisnall commanded the Lancashire contingent at Marston Moor. At one time the credit for having written the journal of the siege was given to Chisnall, on the grounds of his being a known author; he having written a piece of religious polemic called 'A Catholike History'.

There were similarly six named lieutenants of whom, if anything, even less is known than about the captains. They were the Lieutenants Brethergh of Childwall, Penketh of Penketh near Warrington, Walton of Wigan, Worral, Heape and Key of Bury. Whether Edward Halsall was also a lieutenant we do not know, but a note on the fly-leaf of a manuscript copy of the journal of the siege, now in the possession of the British Library, tells us that he was aged seventeen when he was wounded during the siege. He achieved fame in 1650 when he was arrested for the murder of Ascham, parliament's agent in Madrid. He is now generally accepted as being the probable author of the Siege Journal.

Other than these named officers there were three hundred soldiers in the garrison, not all of them being professional soldiers nor members of the militia. Many of Lord Derby's huntsmen, gamekeepers and wildfowlers were pressed into service, their knowledge and skill with firearms making them useful as marksmen and snipers, deployed on the walls and towers to harass the besiegers in their trenches. The domestic staff, who must have been quite numerous, were headed by Mr Broome, Lady Charlotte's Steward.

Prince Rupert of the Rhine, Duke of Cumberland

ALTHOUGH he only enters the scene at the climax of the first siege, and is, therefore, even more peripheral to the main action than is Derby, a word is probably due about Prince Rupert, if only because of his kinship with the countess.

Rupert was the second son of Frederick, King of Bohemia and Elector of the Rhineland Palatinate, by Elizabeth, daughter of James I; thus making Rupert a nephew of Charles I. While Prince Rupert was still a child, his father was driven out of Bohemia by pro-French forces, and the young prince was brought up and educated in the Netherlands, where the family's relationship with the House of Orange-Nassau guaranteed them sanctuary.

Rupert, with his brother Maurice, came to England and joined the king before the raising of the standard at Nottingham in 1642. Rupert proved himself to be a brilliant commander of cavalry, and was arguably the best general the king possessed; certainly in England. In two years he did not lose a battle. Even at Marston, his first and greatest defeat, he proved a match for both Fairfax and the Scots; it was only the Eastern Counties Association's cavalry under Cromwell which defeated him.

In character he was a bundle of contradictions; his good qualities matched by his bad, which were themselves often mirror images of the good so that he was courageous but hot-headed; skilled but impulsive. He could be totally ruthless and could use cruelty as a weapon; yet he could be as equally sentimental and graciously courteous to his enemies.

For Parliament

Sir Thomas Fairfax

IT has to be said at the outset that, although Fairfax was officially responsible for the conduct of siege during the February of 1644, it is by no means certain that he was ever physically present in Lathom. True, he was the commander of the parliamentary forces sent against the house, and he wrote several letters to Lady Derby, which indicate that the direction of negotiations was in his hands. The fact remains that he could just as easily have done all that from a distance, with the colonels on the spot acting as his proxies. Nevertheless, I have taken the fact that he says, in one of his letters, that he will send his coach so that Lady Charlotte might come to New Park for talks with him to mean that he actually was at New Park at the time. And that he was, therefore, present at Lathom, or at least he was there during the first few weeks of the siege.

He was born in 1612 into a prominent Wharfedale family, a member of the West Yorkshire gentry and squirarchy rather than the aristocracy, but well-born and well-connected; his father, Lord Fairfax, was the M.P. for Boroughbridge. Like so many others, he learned the trade of soldiering in the Low Countries, serving under Sir Horace Vere, whose daughter, Anne, he married in 1637. Fairfax himself was an Anglican, but Anne was a strong Presbyterian, and her religious convictions helped influence the direction of his thinking at the onset of the Civil War.

Fairfax was to the fore in the so-called Bishop's Wars in Scotland, for which service he was knighted by the king. Indeed, he stood high in royal favour at this time; for which reason he was chosen by the gentlemen of Yorkshire as the man best fitted to carry their reasonable doubts and grievances to the king. At a muster in York, Fairfax was very publicly snubbed by Charles I, which introduced a coolness between the two men, and which no doubt helped formulate the attitude Fairfax was to take when the quarrel inevitably became civil war. The agonies of conscience suffered by Fairfax are made clear in his writings, but he summarised his personal conclusion as, 'My judgment was for parliament, as the king and kingdom's greatest safeguard.'

In looks he was tall, thin and very dark with what the romantic novelist would call 'saturnine good looks'. There was an air of melancholy in his appearance which, combined with the darkness of his skin and hair, helped give him the nickname 'Black Tom'. In character he was said to be sweet-tempered, mild-mannered and reserved. He was somewhat inarticulate as the result of an extremely bad stutter which tended to overcome him in moments of stress. He was plagued with ill-health, suffering from kidney stone and the pain associated with it, while he had nearly died of smallpox while in the Low Countries in 1631. He seems to have been genuinely likeable, with no-one, not even his enemies, with an ill word to say of him. His equable behaviour did play a significant part in his military success because, as C. V. Wedgwood says, 'His unwillingness to be elated by victory and a stubborn refusal to be cast down by defeat were the great strengths of Fairfax.'

He was a bold and imaginative soldier. It was he, after all, who was chosen to create and establish the New Model Army. His reputation was to be eclipsed by that of Cromwell, but that was not the case during the war. It was only in the political infighting which followed the war that a man of his integrity was lost and he became subservient to Cromwell.

There was one weakness in his character that should have disqualified him from being sent to deal with Lady Derby: being notoriously incapable of being at all severe in his relationship with women. He was known to be dominated by a strong-willed wife, and his daughter was also to prove later that she could twist him round her little finger. In his dealings with Lady Charlotte, he insisted on treating her with the courtesy he felt was the due of all women, and was restricted in his conduct of the siege by a natural reluctance to make war on a woman. It is possibly the case that a man less nice in his attitude to the opposite sex might have dealt more effectively with the taking of the house.

Alexander Rigby M.P.

AS prime mover and only begetter of the siege, Rigby is as central to an understanding of the parliamentary side of this dispute, as Lord Derby is to our understanding of the royalists. Whatever military reasons may have been advanced for the siege to be undertaken, the single-minded pursuit of it by Rigby, and the way in which he sought to resolve it with the maximum amount of damage done to the house and the Stanley family, argues a degree of personal animosity and malice that goes beyond the mere hostility of civil war. According to one unconfirmed report, Rigby was once deeply insulted by James Stanley and sought ever afterwards to be avenged for it. Whatever the truth of that report, there has to be some grudge or resentment eating into Rigby's soul which explains his dedicated vendetta against Lord and Lady Derby and the House itself.

Born in 1594, Rigby's father was a lawyer in Wigan, but Alexander was brought up in Preston. He became a lawyer himself and, in 1638, was known to be living quietly near Kirkham in the Fylde where he became colonel of the Amounderness militia. In 1639 he was jointly elected M.P. for Wigan, alongside the royalist member, Orlando Bridgman. Rigby was re-elected in 1640 with 136 votes, and immediately took a virulently anti-Stanley stance in the new commons, being one of those who were keen to see James Stanley impeached by parliament.

He was a conscientious member, belonging to more committees than any other member of the Long Parliament, commuting between Wigan and Westminster about as frequently, and with as little concern, as an M.P. of today, despite having to do the journey on horseback over virtually non-existent roads. He is described as being a rare combination of energy and talent, who was not always scrupulous. He was not popular; it being said of him that he was, 'admired by many, esteemed by a few, but loved by none.'

He was learned and well-read, owning eighty books at a time when owning one was very rare. From those same books it is clear that he could read, if not speak, French, Latin, Greek and Hebrew. Yet, for all his virtues, there is a cold, unsympathetic feel to his personality. J. J. Bagley, when describing the feelings of his nieces and nephews when Rigby became their guardian in 1644, calls him, 'Serious, forbidding Uncle

Alex; whose sternness and ferocity had become almost legendary.' The picture that emerges is of an extremely intelligent and able man, but one without a redeeming hint of humour or humanity to leaven the obsession that drove him to such a single-minded view of his mission in life. He was a man driven by hate and by anger and by a sense of his own rectitude. A quote from a parliamentary speech he made in 1640 will give the flavour of the man, 'And now shall not some be hanged that have robbed us of all our prosperity – let us not be merciful to those that are merciless to the whole kingdom – Be not pitiful in judgement.'

Thomas Morgan

ALONG with Fairfax, Morgan was the other non-Lancastrian outsider in the forces besieging the house. Born in Llanrhymny in South Wales, in 1604, he was another who had learned the craft of soldiering in the Low Countries. He was a small man, peremptory by nature. He came to the notice of Fairfax at the battle of Nantwich where he commanded the dragoons, but he followed Fairfax to Lathom as artillery officer, and in that capacity he stayed on after Fairfax's departure.

His unfortunate experiences at Lathom did not deter him from pursuing his career with the artillery, and he rose to high rank in the New Model Army following a successful campaign in South Wales, taking in succession the castles of Chepstow, Newport and Raglan.

He became associated with General Monck, and thus became involved in the conspiracy with which Monck and Fairfax instigated the Restoration of Charles II, in 1660; an event which Morgan celebrated by firing a salute from the cannon known as Mons Meg in Edinburgh Castle. Under Charles II, Morgan became governor of Jersey, in 1668, and thereby achieved his niche in history, although his fame has been somewhat overshadowed by his more famous nephew, Henry Morgan, the buccaneer who sacked Panama and was made governor of Jamaica.

Colonel Richard Holland of Heaton

AS head of the parliamentary committee in Manchester, Holland was in the position of being virtual leader of parliamentarian action within the county, and the decision to besiege Lathom House was essentially his, as had been the initial demand for the surrender of the house. Despite his rank of colonel, his main service to parliament in Lancashire was in the capacity of sequestrator rather than as military man.

On the moderate wing of his party, he was one of those who would have sought an accommodation with Lord Derby, or Strange as he then was. On the other hand, he was easily swayed by the more militant hard-liners among the Lancashire leadership, and he is associated with Rigby and Egerton in advocating the sternest of measures to be taken against Lathom House. In the opening months of the war, he was responsible for hiring a German mercenary, named Rosworm, who later claimed to have been cheated of his full salary and took Holland to court for recompense. Much of what we know of Holland's character and behaviour comes from Rosworm's testimony in this case and we must, therefore, bear in mind that our view of Holland is bound to be coloured by the German's dislike and contempt for the man.

Born in 1596, Holland succeeded to his uncle's estates in Denton and Heaton in 1619. He later became colonel of militia for Salford Hundred, a command he surrendered to Peter Egerton when he himself became governor of Manchester and president of the Manchester Committee.

An ineffectual man, his military adventures were not noted for their successes. According to Rosworm, he wanted to surrender Manchester at the first sign of Strange's advance on the town while, in the attack on Wigan, 'he was in such a shaking agony of fear . . . he was ready to march away with all our forces.'

Although Holland initiated the siege, and played a part in the administration of the action, it is virtually certain that he took no part in the military proceedings.

Ralph Assheton of Middleton

THE nearest thing Lancashire produced in the way of a military leader to equal the role of Fairfax in Yorkshire. He was born in 1605, and was a member of the 1640 Parliament as a knight of the shire. He was also the colonel of militia for Blackburn Hundred. As military leader he was responsible for defeating Derby in 1643, and leading the Lancastrian forces which joined Fairfax at Nantwich in January 1644. Assheton's role in the latter fight was highly praised by Fairfax.

Assheton seems to have been highly distrustful of the Holland-Rigby faction on the Manchester Committee and, together with John Moore, appears to have taken up his quarters in Ormskirk rather than stay with Rigby and Egerton at New Park House. Certainly, as will be seen, he quarelled with Rigby and Holland over the conduct of the siege, to the extent of cutting himself off from any further involvement in the conduct of the war.

John Moore of Bank Hall

LEADER of the parliamentary party in Liverpool, he finally succeeded in winning that city for Parliament in 1643, becoming colonel of militia for Derby Hundred. A capable man, he put up a most brilliant defence of Liverpool against Prince Rupert's superior forces in 1644. Like Assheton, he distrusted Rigby and withdrew from the siege at an early date. He was not, however, a moderate man in his opinions, being described as a 'strong puritan, vigorous in the cause'. Alone among the parliamentary leaders I have listed here, he went on to sign the death warrant for Charles I, and thus took his place among the regicides; although he died before Charles II could take his revenge at the Restoration.

Chapter Four

The course of the war in Lancashire prior to June 15 1643

The localised nature of the Civil War

HERE is neither the time nor space to consider the causes of the Civil War in England in a brief, specialised survey such as this. It is a complex subject that hinges on the character of Charles I himself, and on currents and cross-currents of religious and political thought which lie totally outside our experience today – except perhaps in the context of Northern Ireland which remains fossilised in the mixture of religion and politics peculiar to the seventeenth century. To my mind the best survey of the causes of the war remains *The King's Peace* by C. V. Wedgwood, and anyone who wishes to place the struggle in Lancashire within a wider context is advised to consult that work.

On the other hand, there is a very practical reason as to why it is sensible to concentrate on the war in Lancashire, and that is to realise that the Civil War, at least in its opening phases, was not really a national struggle. It was instead a series of localised conflicts in which purely local issues had at least as much importance as any cause of king or parliament. There were some random attempts at inter-county co-operation of which parliament's Eastern Counties Association, based in Cambridge and with Cromwell as its leader, was about the most successful. Other than that, each county produced its own leaders on both sides who conducted their campaigns in their own way and with their own objectives in mind, rather than any national plan.

While we are on this theme, it is worth noting that the political divisions of the Civil War period very seldom have anything to do with the needs, wishes or ambitions of the people as a whole. In many ways the

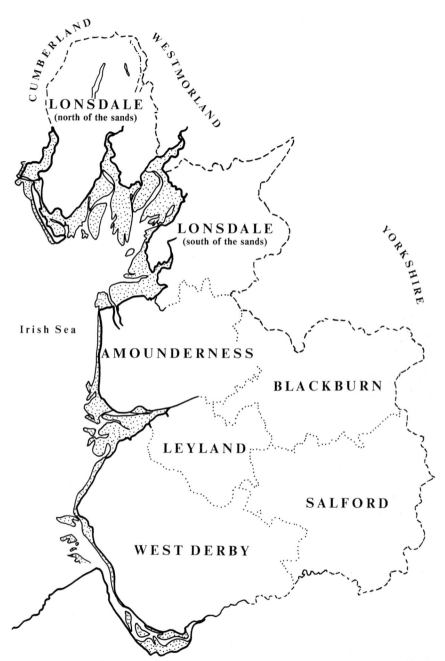

CUMBERLAND

WESTMORLAND

LONSDALE
(north of the sands)

LONSDALE
(south of the sands)

YORKSHIRE

Irish Sea

AMOUNDERNESS

BLACKBURN

LEYLAND

SALFORD

WEST DERBY

A map showing the six Lancashire Hundreds.

feudal system still lived in seventeenth-century England, and the loyalties and allegiances of the ordinary people were decided for them by the local landowners and magnates whose tenants they were. In this way whole counties, dominated by prominent men, as Lancashire had been dominated by the Stanleys, could declare their total support, for one side or the other. At the start of the conflict, the counties of south and eastern England were fairly solid for parliament, while the north and west remained loyal to Charles. In just a handful of counties the disposition of loyalty was not clear-cut and opinion was divided. The position adopted by Lancashire was typical of this.

Lancashire divides fairly neatly into two quite separate entities. In the east of the county lie the textile towns where industry reigned supreme, even in the centuries prior to the Industrial Revolution and the growth of the cotton industry. In the seventeenth century, Lancashire was already a leading producer of fustians and linen. The people who worked in the cloth trade were hard-working, independently minded, progressive and, most importantly, non-conformist by religion. By way of contrast, the west of the county still relied on agriculture and farming, with a people who clung to traditional values and ways of life, a high proportion of them remaining Roman Catholic by religion despite a century of recusancy laws. In England then, as in Northern Ireland at the present, a man's religion decided his politics. The Calvinism of the east supported parliament with vigour; the Roman or Anglican Catholics of the west followed Lord Derby in supporting the king.

The hypothetical line which divided the two religious and political persuasions in the county was, ironically enough, made manifest in the one object of strategic importance the county possessed. This was the road that formed one of the main arteries of communication linking the Midlands and South-West with Scotland. The road entered Lancashire by way of the bridge over the Mersey at Warrington and ran north, through Wigan, to Preston, following the line of the present A49. From Preston, northwards, it followed the route of the A6 through Lancaster, to leave the county in the direction of Kendal, Shap and Carlisle. As has been said, at the beginning of the conflict, those parts of Lancashire east of this road were firmly parliamentarian; those to the west as firmly royalist. The main purpose of both sides, therefore, became either to wrest or maintain control over the four towns – Warrington, Lancaster, Wigan and Preston – which in turn controlled the road. Whichever side could control the road would, in effect, control the county.

It is necessary to add a postscript to say that then, as now, the city of Liverpool was the odd one out; the place that did not fit the pattern. Although located in the royalist west, Liverpool was itself divided into the royalist southern half, led by the Norisses of Speke Hall, and the parliamentarian northern half, led by the Moores of Bank Hall. While the county fought for the road, Liverpudlians fought among themselves for control of the city.

_____

Preliminary rumblings

AS early as 1640 there was discontent with the conduct of James Stanley. In his capacity as Lord Lieutenant and Commissioner of Array, he had raised the county militia to fight in Scotland, in the so-called Bishop's Wars. This had caused resentment, which was only in part about the considerable cost to the county; it was also about the dubious legality of raising the militia for service outside the county for a purpose other than the defence of the county. It was an argument as old as the reluctance of the Anglo-Saxon fyrd to serve outside its native region.

After the wars were over a pamphlet was written, and published in 1642, which accused Lord Strange of illegally raising £20,000 from the county; although the cost had in fact been no more than £4,000, only a third of which was actually raised. Rigby, and others who were voicing these accusations of financial malpractice, also suggested that Strange had somehow interfered in the parliamentary elections of 1640. Months before the war began in earnest, the politically active in Lancashire had divided into factions that were either pro- or anti-Stanley.

This division, between those who were for or against James Stanley, was not necessarily the same as the division between royalist and parliamentarian. In March 1642 the more moderate wing of the parliamentary party approached Lord Strange and asked him to be their leader; a request that he duly rejected. Yet, despite this rejection a dialogue continued between Stanley and this group; he, hoping that they might be reconciled with the king, while they in turn trusted that he might be persuaded to transfer his allegiance to their cause, especially when a series of acts, which were insensitive at best, showed the distrust in which the king held the Stanley family. No allegiances changed as the result of these contacts but the dialogue did continue, almost to the last minute.

By the summer of 1642 it had become evident that the country was sliding inexorably into war. Lord Strange decided that he should use his influence in the county to ensure that Lancashire declared for the king. In association with John Girlington, in his capacity as the Commissioner of Array, he called the county to a muster at Preston on June 20th, reading out his commission and asking the men of Lancashire to bear arms for their king. The muster was countered by a group led by Alexander Rigby and Richard Shuttleworth, whose aim was to break up the meeting before any firm commitment could be made in support of the king.

Rigby described the consequent disturbance in a letter he wrote to the Speaker . . . 'The High Sheriff exhibited the commission of array and exclaimed 'For the King, For the King'. On which about 400 joined in the exclamation but the others prayed for King and Parliament.' As a result of this evidence of divided opinion in the county, Stanley took possession of stands of arms in Preston, Warrington and Liverpool in the name of the king, but was unable to do likewise in Manchester, where Rigby and Shuttleworth had anticipated his actions and denied him access.

On July 15, the moderate faction sought to defuse the increasingly volatile situation by inviting Lord Strange to come to Manchester for discussions. This he did, and discussions over a meal were proceeding in an apparently cordial manner, until the fact of his presence became known, and a hostile crowd gathered outside the rooms where the meeting was taking place. At first merely threatening, the behaviour of this crowd deteriorated until it had all the characteristics of a lynch mob, and Stanley was forced to break off the meeting and flee for his life; taking refuge from his pursuers in the Radcliffe home at Ordsall. Even though there remained those who hoped for a non-violent solution, the opinions of the rank and file had obviously hardened beyond the point where reconciliation was possible.

From Manchester, Strange moved to Warrington, where he joined three other leading royalist figures – Lord Molyneux, Sir Thomas Tyledesley and Gilbert Gerard. Together, the four men had assembled a force which must have numbered between three and four thousand. Ignore a statement in the *County History,* repeated by Padfield in *A History of Ormskirk,* which states that James Stanley raised 20,000 men from the area. It is doubtful whether there were more than 20,000 in arms for the king in the country as a whole. At some point in history an extra '0' has been added to the two thousand men which was probably Lord Strange's personal contribution to the force gathered at Warrington.

The four leaders wrote to the king, stating their preparedness and declaring that they believed they had a largely loyal county. If the king were to raise his standard and declare a state of war, then their considered opinion was that he would be best to do that in Lancashire. Given the divisions which had already appeared, and allowing for anti-royalist feelings being very strong in the Manchester area, Charles is hardly to be blamed for ignoring this suggestion. Nevertheless, it was seen as the first of many royal snubs to Stanley when, on August 22nd, the king chose to raise his standard in defiance at Nottingham.

Stanley loses a battle, gains a title and then loses an army

ON September 16, 1642, parliament issued the articles of impeachment against James Stanley, which cited those same complaints that had been made against him in 1640, namely the misuse of moneys, the illegal use of the county militia and interference in the elections. Since he and they were now on opposing sides in a real war, it is hard to see what purpose was served by parliament's motion of impeachment, except that it lent some legitimacy to the measures Rigby, and others, proposed to take against the Stanley family in Lancashire.

Whether in response to the impeachment, or, more likely, out of a sense of resentment at the ill-treatment he had received at the hands of the Manchester mob in July, Lord Strange moved immediately onto the offensive, leading his forces against Manchester, as the centre of the parliamentary organisation for the county. Given the lack of preparedness of the Manchester Committee, and the pusillanimity of men such as Holland, Strange did not expect much in the way of opposition. In fact, the Manchester Committee had hurriedly obtained the services of a German mercenary, Rosworm, who had gained considerable experience in the continental wars. According to his own account, later, it was Rosworm himself who stiffened the resistance of the Manchester men, where they would have surrendered if left to their own devices.

Strange was prevented from entering Manchester, and his forces were pinned down outside the Salford Gate. Unable to believe that the Mancunians were capable of resisting him, and thinking that the first repulse was a fluke, Lord Strange settled down outside the town where he established a form of siege which lasted for about a week. The people of Manchester showed no signs of being intimidated, and a succession of attacks by Strange's soldiers were quite easily driven off.

What could well have become a long drawn-out stalemate was broken by an event quite unrelated to the war. On September 28th, the death occurred of William Stanley, sixth Earl of Derby, and James Stanley, as a result, inherited the title as seventh earl. There was, in fact, no real change in his circumstances since he had filled the earl's offices for many years, but the complications attendant upon his father's death at this confused time left the new earl incapable of concentrating on his siege of Manchester. On the 30th of the month, the new Lord Derby broke off the engagement and withdrew his forces from the Manchester area.

There then followed one of those instances of the distrust in which the king held James Stanley and the spiteful way he had of showing it. Claiming that Derby was unlikely to be totally committed to the king's cause in the circumstances, he removed Stanley from the command of the Lancashire forces. A number of those forces were left under the command of Sir Thomas Tyledesley; although sent to serve in Cheshire. But, many of the Lancashire men were sent much further afield. According to regimental records quoted by Mike Lawson in his book *For God and the North,* a substantial proportion of the men raised by James Stanley in the early days of the war ended their service in the outlying regiments and garrisons protecting the king's headquarters in Oxford.

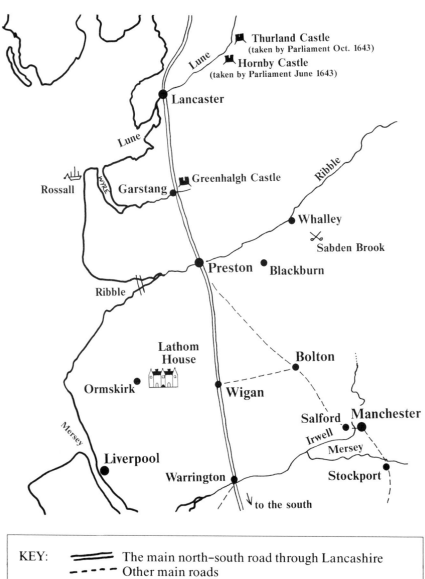

Thurland Castle
(taken by Parliament Oct. 1643)

Hornby Castle
(taken by Parliament June 1643)

Lancaster

Lune

Rossall
Garstang
Greenhalgh Castle
Ribble

Whalley
Sabden Brook

Ribble
Preston
Blackburn

Lathom
House
Bolton

Ormskirk
Wigan

Salford Manchester
Irwell
Mersey

Liverpool

Warrington
Stockport
to the south

KEY:
The main north–south road through Lancashire
Other main roads
Houses or castles held for the king
Battle of Sabden Brook, April 1643
Wreck of Spanish ship off Rossall
Horse ford across the Ribble

Map showing the principal places associated with the war, 1642-3.

In October, Derby did put out tentative peace feelers, but even the moderate wing of the parliamentary party refused to treat with him; if moderation had ever existed it had withered and died during the attack on Manchester.

Hostilities begin and Derby loses another army

WITH Derby's forces thus dispersed or disbanded, the parliamentary leaders made the most of their opportunities in the new year of 1643, and began the moves which they hoped would lead to control of the high road, and thereby of the county itself.

In quick succession, during February and March of the new year, the towns of Preston, Wigan and Lancaster fell to parliamentary forces, of which Ralph Assheton was now acknowledged leader. In March Lord Derby attempted a counter-attack, leading a small force of cavalry northward across the Ribble, by-passing Preston by using the horse-ford between Hesketh Bank and Freckleton.

On his way north, Derby's attention was distracted by a Spanish ship which had come ashore near Fleetwood. He was determined that any armaments which might be on the vessel should not fall into the hands of parliament, and ordered the Spanish crew to abandon ship, despite their real hopes of refloating her. Once they were out of the way, Derby did his best to destroy both ship and guns. In this he failed, although he did manage to incapacitate the ship to the extent that she would never sail again. The sum total of his achievement was that he had deprived the Spanish crew of their ship and wasted his own time, and to no good purpose since the parliamentarians took all the guns from the wreck as soon as Derby had retired.

From Fleetwood Derby moved on to Lancaster. There he could do no more than burn the suburbs since he was unable to dislodge the garrison from the castle. When Assheton advanced from Preston to the relief of Lancaster, Derby was forced to retreat. In the event, however, the sense of blundering mismanagement which characterises this early stage of the war, transferred itself from Derby to Assheton. In recruiting this relief column for Lancaster, Assheton had stripped Preston of its parliamentary garrison. As Derby fell back in the face of Assheton's advance he found Preston undefended. It was a simple matter to occupy the town and reclaim it for the king. And, at almost the same moment, Sir Thomas Tyledesley, re-entering the county with his Lancashire men, moved up from Warrington to re-take Wigan.

After three months of manoeuvring, therefore, the situation had reverted almost to the status quo of the previous year, except that

Lancaster remained in the hand of parliament. In the meantime, Lord Derby had raised yet another army from his estates, producing, it was claimed, no fewer than 5,000 men. It was stated, however, that these were mere 'naked men' – not in the literal sense, of course, but in the sense of being men without arms or equipment. In another account they are said to be 'club-men'. Without proper arms, and being late, reluctant and impressed men, they were unlikely despite their numbers, to represent a military threat of any magnitude.

It was with this makeshift army, stiffened by as many cavalry and trained soldiers as could be spared, that Derby set out up the Ribble Valley from Preston in April. It was essentially a feint, because the plan was to outflank the main parliamentary force around Blackburn and then to strike for the parliamentary heartland in central and eastern Lancashire. Having followed the Ribble as far as Whalley, he crossed the Calder and established a base in the grounds of Whalley Abbey. He intended to head south from here towards Burnley, but, for the moment, he left the raw recruits, with the artillery, in the Abbey grounds, while he himself, with his trained soldiers and cavalry forming a vanguard, led the way up the Padiham road out of Whalley, heading towards Read.

Assheton had anticipated all of Derby's moves, and his men from the Blackburn militia had lined the hedgerows along the road Derby was now following. With the royalist army strung out along the road out of the valley, Assheton's musketeers suddenly opened fire, pouring in volley after volley of enfilading fire from their prepared positions. It was all too much and too sudden for Derby's rank and file, 'No commands of officers nor force of horsemen could make them turn or stay – but gone they would be,' as an eye-witness said.

The vanguard retreated in complete confusion, hastening back down the valley towards Whalley. Local people, alerted by the noise, came out of their houses and assisted in the pursuit. The fleeing vanguard streamed back, through the artillery park near the Abbey, creating an even greater panic among the untrained men. 'The remnant of this army likewise turned their backs and fled.' Within a matter of minutes all that Derby had gained had been lost.

From victory at Whalley, Assheton moved on Preston which he re-took without opposition. As the news spread of Derby's defeat and the fall of Preston to Assheton, Holland advanced on Wigan. Tyledesley, menaced on all sides, recognised the impossibility of maintaining his hold on the town, levelled the town-walls, and retired to join Derby. The two men, together with Molyneux and as many cavalry as they could salvage from these defeats, then retired to York to consult with the Queen who represented her husband in the North.

On May 27th, Booth succeeded in capturing Warrington, and from that moment the whole of Lancashire was in the hands of parliament with the exceptions of royalist garrisons at Lathom, Greenhalgh near Garstang, and at Hornby and Thurland Castles in Lonsdale.

In York, James Stanley did his best to persuade the Queen, Henrietta Maria, to send help to the beleaguered royalists of Lancashire; a plea which was soon to be reinforced by a similar message from Lady Derby. Henrietta Maria was not interested in supporting the Stanley influence in Lancashire, however; she had a more important mission for Derby to perform.

There was now a real risk that the Scots would make a common cause with the English parliament; an alliance in effect of two branches of Presbyterianism. If that were to happen, the Scots would, no doubt, look seriously at the prospect of regaining the Isle of Man, traditionally subject to the Scottish Crown but held, in fact, by the Stanley family since the fifteenth century. The prospect of Scottish allies of parliament using the Isle of Man as a base from which they could raid the English and Welsh coasts and threaten the link with Ireland, was a serious threat to the royalist cause. In the name of the king, Queen Henrietta Maria ordered Derby to go and secure his Manx possessions in the king's interest.

Derby had no option but to acquiesce, but he went first to Lathom where, as he later wrote, 'having secretly made what provision I possibly could of men, arms and ammunition, for the defence and protection of my wife and children against the insolence and affronts of the enemy. . . (I) . . . prepared for my speedy passage to the Isle of Man.' By the 'provision of men', Derby presumably meant that he left with his wife those officers and men who remained with him after the debacle at Whalley. Certainly the Captains Ratcliffe, Chisnall and Rawstorne, who had been with Derby at Preston in April, now transferred to officer the garrison. Derby did not have long to make these preparations because we know that he arrived in the Isle of Man on June 15th. With Derby's removal to his island possessions, the first phase of the Civil War in Lancashire can be said to have ended, the spotlight turning away from Derby himself and onto his wife. The siege of Lathom House had begun.

Part Two

The first siege

Chapter Five

May 27, 1643 – February 24, 1644
Rigby's initiative

MMEDIATELY after the taking of Warrington, with the four principal towns along the road in their hands, with Derby, Tyledesley and Molyneux out of the county in York, and with the royalist armies dispersed and beaten, the committee of the holy state in Manchester could easily feel justified in believing that the war in Lancashire was over, with parliament triumphant. In his capacity as sequestrator for the county Richard Holland wrote to Lady Derby requiring that she should either, compound by accepting the supremacy of parliament, or she should surrender up the house and estates.

The countess refused, saying that, 'As she had not lost her regard for the Church of England, nor her allegiance to her Prince, nor her faith to her Lord, she could not therefore, as yet, give up the house. They must never hope to gain it, until she had, either lost all these (three), or her life in defence of them.'

Notwithstanding her defiance of Holland's demands, Lady Charlotte sent word to her husband and also communicated to the Queen her urgent need of help and reinforcement if she was to withstand the pressure to surrender the house; claiming that she needed 3,000 men to defend the house adequately. It was much the same message as Derby had been putting forward, and it met with no more success. The only help given to Lady Derby was the brief visit of her husband before he went on to the Isle of Man.

The result of Derby's visit to Lathom en route for the Isle of Man, was the installation of a garrison of three hundred men, one tenth of the number Lady Derby had said she needed. In terms of armaments the house was provided with six sakers, which are small cannon, more often found on board ship; two sling-pieces; wide-mouthed cannon, which fired stone rather than lead shot; and a collection of murderers, which were even smaller guns, sometimes known as swivel-guns, and used at close-range to disperse a crowd of attackers. The garrison was not large, and nor was it a very fearsome armoury. To add to these difficulties there was a constant shortage of powder and ammunition. During the siege, a total of seven barrels of powder were used, but this was only possible thanks to the replenishment of supplies in raids on the besiegers. It was a constant fear on the part of those in the house, that they would not be able to withstand a determined assault through lack of ammunition and fire-power. The main cause of the garrison's success in withstanding the siege, was the bluff by which they convinced their enemies that their strength was greater than it was in fact.

By mid-summer, no active move had been made against Lathom, although a state of siege had in effect come into being as soon as Holland had demanded the house's surrender. The intention of the parliamentarians to take the house had been announced and, from that moment, Lady Derby and her garrison were confined to the house and grounds by the need to keep it constantly defended. And yet, once the summons had been issued, and their intention to sequestrate had been made known, the Manchester committee seemed to lose all interest in Lathom. It was as though they realised that Lathom posed no real threat to the county's security and could safely be ignored till they had the time, the motivation and the manpower to do something about it.

When action was taken it was as a result of individual initiative, rather than because of a decision by the committee. It was Alexander Rigby who took it upon himself to see to the reduction of the last few royalist strongholds remaining in Lancashire. During the summer, Rigby began to move his men into the environs of the royalist enclaves where they could harass the garrisons. During that autumn he was partially rewarded by the surrender of the Lonsdale castles at Hornby and Thurland. At Lathom he was not so successful.

It was not an all-out investment which was pursued at this point. Rigby's efforts consisted rather of a presence in the area which could mount patrols with the objects, on the one hand of keeping her ladyship and her garrison penned up within the grounds of the house, and on the other of preventing supplies from reaching the garrison from outside. In this latter purpose he was singularly ineffective, because supplies of food at least continued to be taken into the house despite the patrols. It was the degree of success on the part of the garrison in obtaining these supplies from the surrounding district that was no doubt responsible for Rigby's describing the garrison, in his letters to the committee in Manchester, as a 'nest of brigands' which was despoiling the countryside.

One has to feel sorry for the people of Ormskirk and district. On the one hand they had been tenants or loyal supporters of the Stanley family for generations; they would feel obliged to render their dues when asked. Yet simultaneously they were at the mercy of Rigby's men, who were, no doubt, living 'off the country' as it was euphemistically called, and who, probably, accused as guilty of treason anyone who gave so much as a loaf to the Lathom garrison. As is so often the case, the innocent bystander was caught between two fires, and was forced to pay their dues twice over.

In such a manner, matters proceeded through the autumn and into the winter. In his reports to Manchester, Rigby claimed to have kept Lady Charlotte 'warded up', not necessarily kept to the house, but certainly contained within the boundaries of the estate. At the same time he lost no opportunity for complaining vigorously to Manchester about the garrison; it was a 'nest of brigands', it was a base from which these men 'terrorised and despoiled' the neighbourhood; it was, above all, a threat to the security of the county. Rigby appealed for help in the reduction of the garrison and urged that serious steps were taken that would enforce the surrender of the house. For a long time there was a noticeable lack of response to these appeals but, during the month of January, 1644, a sequence of apparently unconnected events combined to produce a situation that would change the course of the siege.

The origin of that series of events lies in the Irish Question. A steady flow of Irish soldiers, under the command of Ormonde, was being directed into England through the port of Chester. These Irish levies, which now formed a significant part of the royalist forces, were hated intensely by the parliamentarians with whom the Irish were religiously incompatible. Moreover, the recent troubles in Ulster had led to many atrocity stories concerning the treatment of protestant settlers which in turn led to the generally-held belief that the Irish were cruel and barbarous in their treatment of women and prisoners. A policy of 'no-quarter, no-prisoners' applied to Irish combatants. It also became a matter of some urgency to the parliamentary command that the influx of royalist Irish should be stopped, and the line of communication between Chester and the Midlands be cut.

The Irish threat was such that it broke down the county divisions, and a co-ordinated strategy was finally evolved by parliament. It was as part of this strategy that Sir Thomas Fairfax, as Commander in the North for parliament, was sent west of the Pennines to co-operate with the parliamentary forces of the North-West and North Midlands in order to deal with this problem of the Irish. With Cheshire firmly loyal to the king, Fairfax was forced to work from the Manchester area, leaning quite strongly on Assheton's support in the action which followed. On January 24, 1644, Fairfax and his forces met a combined Irish-royalist army at Nantwich and totally defeated them.

C. V. Wedgwood described Fairfax after Nantwich as being, 'ill with cold and worry, uncertain about the future.' He did not doubt that the mission he had carried out at Nantwich was important, but he did fret about being delayed west of the Pennines when matters in Yorkshire had reached a critical point. The main Yorkshire army, under his father, Lord Fairfax, was bottled up in Hull by Belasyse, while the Scots, who had finally invaded in support of the English parliament, were held up at Chester-le-Street in County Durham, faced by Lord Newcastle. If the two armies could evade their respective opponents and combine into one major force, they would ensure the supremacy of parliament in the North of England. Fairfax could see this; could fret at the delay in bringing it about; and, above all, wanted to be there in Yorkshire to make it happen. Unfortunately, he was prevented from returning to his home county by the weather. During that January there had been seven days of continuous snowfall. By the time Fairfax's service at Nantwich was done, not a pass through the Pennines remained open. Perforce he had to remain in Lancashire.

The problems of the Irish, together with bad weather, had combined to provide the first of the circumstances which led to a change in the management of the siege of Lathom House; the presence in Lancashire of a senior, skilled and experienced military commander.

Also in January, a troop of Rigby's horse, commanded by a Captain Hindley, on patrol in the vicinity of Lathom House, had come across a party of Derby sympathisers, who were attempting to smuggle provisions or armaments into the house. Hindley immediately took the group into custody, and was escorting them into detention when they, in turn, were attacked by a party drawn from the Lathom garrison. The small troop of parliamentary horse were unable to prevent the rescue of the prisoners and, indeed, some of the group – a Lieutenant Dandy along with several troopers – were taken prisoner in their turn.

For Rigby it was the final straw. He went personally to Manchester in order to browbeat the committee with a long catalogue of complaints about aggression from the House which had culminated in this last most serious attack. The burden of his complaint was clear; Lathom House had been under threat of sequestration since the previous May, it had been partially blockaded since then, but not at the request of the Manchester committee, who had done absolutely nothing, while the garrison continued to offer provocation after provocation. Now the garrison had taken military action against the soldiers of parliament, and could no longer be ignored. It was time for the committee to do what it should have done from the first and issue orders for the house to be reduced, by force if necessary.

The coincidence of this appeal being made to Manchester, at the very moment that they had the services of the northern commander to dispose of, was too great to be overlooked by Holland and company. On Saturday February 24th, 1644, after protracted discussions, the Council of the Holy State in Manchester issued orders that Sir Thomas Fairfax, aided by colonels Rigby, Moore and Assheton, with a force of 3,000 men and a train of artillery, was to seek the submission of Lathom House. This was to be accompanied by negotiation if possible, but by force if need be.

Fairfax was reluctant, partly because of his need to return to the situation in Yorkshire, and partly because he saw no particular purpose that would be served by making a heavy military commitment to reduce a house of no particular military importance. However, the orders given by the Committee of Both Kingdoms, when he had been sent to Lancashire in the first place, had been that he should assist the parliamentarian cause in Lancashire in whatever way they saw best. This was now to be treated as the official sanction for putting him in charge of the army that was to move against Lathom. According to Bagley it was, in fact, Fairfax who persuaded the Manchester committee to take action against Lathom and Greenhalgh, against their better judgement. All the evidence I have been able to find, however, points to the reverse being true.

Chapter Six

February 25 - March 6, 1644
Fairfax in command
- the futile negotiations

ROM here on we are totally dependent on the diarist who wrote the journal of the siege to discover the course of events. There are other accounts of the siege, from writers on both sides of the conflict, and these are more fully evaluated in the bibliography. But these accounts are even more biased - even while cancelling each other out - and they are very often, probably, inaccurate in the dates quoted and even in the chronology of events. Not that the diarist is perfect since there can be no doubt that the diarist is distinctly one-sided in his bias; this is evident in his version of the fortunes of war prior to the start of the siege in which, to quote a more recent authority, he was 'economical with the truth.' In this version, Lord Derby's successes are magnified and his failures ignored. There is no reason to doubt that a similar edited version of the truth is what we have in the journal.

Nevertheless, however biased the account may be, it is the only eye witness, blow-by-blow history that we have. As long as we are prepared to take the diarist's observations with a healthy pinch of salt we can accept it as a reasonably accurate timetable of events. The story that follows is based very closely on the journal, though I am prepared to editorialise when the bias becomes a little too blatant.

Lady Derby heard a garbled account of the meeting in Manchester on the morning of Sunday the 25th and, at once, according to the diarist, despatched a messenger to 'her secret friend, one acquainted with their deliberations'. This is the first of several hints that Lady Derby had a spy in the enemy camp, someone close to the leaders of the besieging forces who was sufficiently well-inclined towards Lord and Lady Derby as to be prepared to betray the secret plans of the besiegers. It is certainly true that Lady Derby had very good intelligence of the other side's intentions during the negotiations that followed, although that intelligence did decrease after both Moore and Assheton left the siege in early April, suggesting that Lady Derby's informant was an officer with one of these two colonels.

Her messenger returned to the house on Monday, able to confirm that the council had ordered action to be taken against the house, and that soldiers led by Fairfax were already on the road from Manchester. The route taken by this army was said to be by way of Bolton and Wigan and then via Standish; the last-named being somewhat out of the way to the north. The interpretation put on this detour by the diarist is that a feint was intended so that people would believe that Lathom House was not the destination of the army but that, in marching north from Wigan, they were heading for Westmoreland and a union with the Scots. It is highly unlikely that such a cumbersome move would have fooled anybody nor that such a deception was either needed or intended. A much more likely explanation of the detour by way of Standish is that the direct road from Wigan to Lathom crosses the ridge between Ashurst Beacon and Billinge Hill, and the slopes were likely to be too steep for the artillery train. By diverting to Standish it would be possible to use the gentler gradients of Wrightington Moor and the Douglas Valley.

As a matter of fact, there was little purpose in seeking to hide the destination of the army. Any desire for secrecy, if such desire there was, was quite negated by the actions of the Rev. James Bradshaw, the reforming minister imposed upon Wigan parish church when parliamentary forces took the town. Perhaps inspired by having his party's leaders in the congregation, he chose to preach his sermon to a text taken from Jeremiah, chapter 50, verse 14 – 'Put yourselves in array against Babylon round about: all ye that bend the bow shoot at her, spare no arrows; for she hath sinned against the Lord.' Oblivious of any need for secrecy, Bradshaw equated Babylon itself with Lathom House and Lady Derby with the Whore of Babylon, the Scarlet Woman. If his congregation had not known what was intended when his sermon began they were surely in no doubt by the time he had finished, concluding as he did with the statement that he intended to reserve the next verse for the day of victory. That verse reads, 'Shout against her round about, her foundations are fallen, her walls are thrown down, for it is the vengeance of the Lord.'

The besieging forces took up their positions before Lathom House on Tuesday the 27th. There is no clear picture of their disposition, the diarist merely saying that they made their quarters at the distance of 'a mile – two or three at the furthest.' Seacome, on the other hand, while failing to mention where the rank and file soldiers were based, states quite definitely that Fairfax, with his senior officers, made Ormskirk his headquarters. Evidence of the 'Cromwell Stone' would suggest that the main parliamentary camp was in the Tawd Valley, while the wording of the journal makes it clear that the forward base for the parliamentary officers was New Park House. The distances involved are not totally incompatible with the diarist's statements. Both the site of the 'Cromwell Stone' and New Park are about three-quarters of a mile from Lathom House, and Ormskirk is about two and a half miles away.

Fairfax was not a lover of sieges; throughout his military career he avoided them wherever possible and, when the taking of any fortified place was necessary, he tended to favour an immediate assault in order to take the place by storm, believing that the inevitable high cost in casualties was worth it if it avoided the constant drain on resources, money and morale during a long, drawn-out siege of attrition. In this Fairfax was normally both determined and quite ruthless. That he did not immediately advocate a similar solution for Lathom House can only be because of an inherent reluctance to be seen waging war on a woman. Throughout his time in charge of the siege he attempted to resolve the matter through negotiation; and persisted with that even after it was made clear that Lady Derby was just not going to surrender tamely, and that she was considerably more adroit at exploiting the situation than were Fairfax's negotiators.

Negotiations began almost at once with a Captain Markland arriving at the house on Wednesday morning in order to present Lady Derby with a copy of a parliamentary ordinance and a personal letter from Fairfax. The ordinance was very much a re-wording of Holland's request for the surrender of the house made the previous year, but this time with the full backing of parliament, and urging the Countess of Derby to listen sympathetically to any proposals put by Sir Thomas Fairfax. Both Lord and Lady Derby were assured of the most merciful of treatment, if they would surrender and compound with parliament. The letter from Fairfax which accompanied this ordinance, promised all the help that Sir Thomas could give in securing the best possible terms from parliament. 'Madam I do owe you that so much honour as a Lady that I should use all just means that would make me capable of serving your Ladyship.'

Still in the excess of courtesy in which these exchanges were conducted, Lady Charlotte replied that:

She much wondered that Sir Thos. Fairfax would require her to give up her Lord's house without any offence on her part done to the Parliament: desiring in a business of such weight that struck both at her religion and her life, that so nearly concerned her Sovereign, her Lord and her whole Posterity, she might have a week's consideration both to resolve the doubts of her conscience, and to seek advice on matters of law and honour.

As the diarist freely admits, Lady Charlotte's conscience did not admit to any doubts, nor did she require any advice on law or honour; the request for a week's grace was merely an attempt to buy time. That much was immediately obvious to Fairfax who, in rejecting her request out of hand, made the counter-suggestion that the countess should come by coach to New Park House where she could discuss the matter face-to-face with himself and his colonels.

Such a suggestion met with no more favour from her ladyship and, in the haughty tones of offended dignity, she replied, 'Say to Sir Thomas Fairfax that, notwithstanding my present condition, I shall not forget either the honour of my Lord or my own birth. And that I conceive it more knightly that Sir Thomas Fairfax should wait upon me than I upon him.' It rapidly became clear that, even if Fairfax was not going to give her her week's grace as of right, she would take it nevertheless by the time-wasting tactics of these futile points of order and precedence. Having wasted Wednesday in the exchanges reported above, both Thursday and Friday were spent in the to and fro exchange of even more letters and messages. Virtually nothing was accomplished by this. An exchange of prisoners was arranged but, by the evening of Friday, March the first, Fairfax was so frustrated by the lack of progress, that he demanded the right to safe conduct for two of his colonels to come to the house for face-to-face consultations. To which Lady Derby finally did agree.

Colonels Assheton and Rigby went to the house on Saturday, the second of March. Lady Charlotte received them with a complete change of tactics in that, up until then she had maintained what might be called 'a very low profile', representing herself as weak and defenceless. Now, in a complete contrast, she made great play with as many of her garrison as possible; mounting a guard of honour, both in the inner courtyard and in the Great Hall, manning all the towers and deploying all the cannon in an attempt to impress the visitors with the numbers and strength of the defenders. The countess herself received the two men in the Great Chamber of Presence, seated on a throne-like chair, with her ladies-in-waiting about her and her two young daughters at her feet. The whole intention was to over-awe the two colonels, impress on them the strong position of the defenders, and to belittle whatever proposals they may have to offer.

Fairfax asked for the surrender of the house, subject to four conditions:

Firstly, all arms and ammunition in the house were to be surrendered to Sir Thomas Fairfax immediately.

Secondly, Lady Charlotte, and those people with her, were free to leave the house, taking all their possessions with them, and were free to go to Chester or any other town in royalist hands. Alternatively, the lady's supporters could compound with parliament and go to their own homes, it being understood that, in so doing, they would have given their parole not to take up arms again in opposition to parliament.

Thirdly, as it affected the countess herself, she could, if she chose, retire to Knowsley with her menial (rather than her military) servants, and be permitted to live there with a maximum of twenty musketeers for her defence. Or again, if she so wished, she could join her husband in the Isle of Man.

Fourthly, the countess would be allowed to keep those lands, and – more importantly – the revenues, that belonged to her husband in the Hundred of West Derby. This, however, was a provisional agreement, and was to be conditional upon approval by parliament. But Fairfax, and the other leaders, would do all in their power to persuade parliament to continue this allowance.

In many ways these were very favourable terms and, given the relative strengths of the besieging and defending forces, amounted to concessions on Fairfax's part. Lady Derby, however, was determined not to accept them and seized upon the fourth and final condition as being in part dishonourable, in part uncertain. That which had to be confirmed by parliament could, quite as easily, be revoked by parliament. It was impossible to negotiate in any meaningful fashion if they had to refer back to parliament every suggestion they put forward. If they were to get anywhere, they should first of all go back to parliament and learn from them exactly what it was that could be offered. Then they could work on an established basis and everything would go more smoothly. On the other hand, she summed up, that would seem to be a great deal of trouble to put them to. She had no real wish that the good gentlemen should have to put themselves out on her behalf. Would it not be much better, and far less trouble, if the army withdrew and she were allowed to go on as she had been doing, minding her own business, causing no trouble for anyone?

Far from being over-awed by the reception they had been given, the two colonels went so far as to argue with Lady Derby, taking her up on the point of her being no trouble to anyone, and taxed her with all the trouble caused to the surrounding countryside by her soldiers and servants. She in turn replied that she could look after her own, and said that they might look in their own ranks for the trouble-makers, citing ministers and preachers who sowed discord by preaching the downfall of noble families, and even advocating the overthrow of the king. Here she was referring specifically to Henry Marten, who had been expelled from the House of Commons in August, 1643, for proposing the deposition of King Charles. She culminated by making the divisive point that the two colonels should take Sir Thomas Fairfax as their example because he, a gentleman, would never allow such talk.

All that emerged from the meeting was an agreement that she in her turn, would present her counter-proposals, if someone came to receive them on the following Monday. She also managed to convey the message that Assheton would be welcome as this recipient, but that Rigby would not.

The Sunday being spent in prayer by both sides, it was Monday when Assheton went to the house alone, as proposed, to receive Lady Derby's counter-proposals, and was received by the lady with rather less ceremony than had been shown on the Saturday. The countess had drawn up a list of four points to mirror the four conditions suggested by Fairfax for the house's surrender.

Firstly, she requested a month of 'quiet continuance' at Lathom, after which time she, together with her children, friends, soldiers and servants, with all their goods, arms and cannon, should have free transit to the Isle of Man. During that month she should be allowed to keep a garrison within her house for her defence.

Secondly, she promised that none of her arms would be used against the parliament, either while she was still in the country or after she had left for the Isle of Man.

Thirdly, during her month's stay at Lathom no soldiers should be quartered on the Derby estates, either at Lathom or Knowsley.

Fourthly, she required re-assurances that no-one who had supported her would suffer for having given that support, once she had left.

Not one of these conditions, except for the fourth, meant exactly what it said; as was freely admitted by the diarist. In the first she was merely seeking to win more time, in the hope that external factors might begin to move in her favour. By 'Parliament' in the second, she did not mean the elected parliament at Westminster but, the 'Parliament of the Three Estates', the continental-style assembly set up by Charles I in Oxford to act as his puppet council. In the third condition she was seeking to clear the environs of the house so as to replenish her supplies.

None of these equivocations fooled Thomas Fairfax for one moment; he knew them at once for what they were. He did not, however, make the mistake of rejecting them out of hand. On the contrary, he did accept them as far as the countess, her family, friends and other non-combatants were concerned. He did, however, exempt the cannon from the arms she would be allowed to take to the Isle of Man, and he required that a parliamentary officer with forty men should replace her garrison, the soldiers of which should be disbanded by ten o'clock of the following morning.

The messenger chosen to acquaint Lady Charlotte with these amendments was Thomas Morgan, Fairfax's artillery officer, described by the diarist as insolent and peremptory in manner. Since Lady Derby had not been sincere in the terms she had offered, she had no hesitation in rejecting those terms, as amended by Fairfax. Indeed, recognising that she had reached the end of her delaying tactics, she sought a psychological advantage by turning the argument around so as to represent the amendments made by Fairfax as outright rejection; claiming to be glad of it, in one of the histrionic speeches with which she dramatised her role throughout the siege.

> She refused all their articles, and was truly happy they had refused hers, protesting she had rather hazard her life than offer their like again. That

though a woman and a foreigner divorced from her friends and robbed of her estate, she was ready to receive their utmost violence, trusting in God both for protection and deliverance.

Morgan attempted to point out the weakness of her position by using his knowledge of artillery to outline the power of the cannons, mortar and engineering works to be employed against her. Then he withdrew to repeat her answer to his superiors. The response was not unexpected.

The visit by Morgan was the last step in the process of negotiation, at least as far as Fairfax was concerned. It is stated by Seacome that Fairfax was recalled from Lathom, for service elsewhere, on Wednesday March 6th, and that the command of the siege then devolved upon Peter Egerton, colonel of Salford Hundred. The diarist is less clear about any change of command, and Egerton is not mentioned; but then there is every indication that Lady Derby's intelligence for this period is not as complete as it had been. We know, for example, that it is not until the garrison was able to question prisoners taken during a skirmish on March 12th, that they learned the outcome of a council of war that had taken place before Fairfax's departure; that is, on March 5th or 6th.

That council of war was convened to decide what course of action to take after the obvious failure of negotiation. It was now clear that the lady was not going to give up the house without a struggle, and it was necessary to decide what tactics to employ as an alternative. The cannon had not yet been brought up and could not be used. And, in any case, Morgan was probably well aware of the limitations that would be placed on the artillery because of the topography of the site, which left just two alternatives; either the house could be stormed, using a petard to blow in the gates and then rushing the garrison. Or a true siege and investment could be mounted, with the object of starving the garrison into submission. With the benefit of hindsight, we know that the former expedient would have been very likely to have succeeded. It is true that the attackers might have suffered heavy casualties, but a ratio in their favour of ten attackers to one defender would have been enough to have ensured the inevitable victory of the attackers. At the same time, our hindsight enables us to know that the garrison had sufficient food stocks in the house to have lasted them until July, so that there never was, in fact, any possibility of starving them out.

According to Seacome, Fairfax was opposed to the idea of an assault on the house – 'he declared himself against a present storm (urged by some) and advised a regular siege.' If this is true, it conflicts with Fairfax's behaviour later and his known dislike for the siege of attrition as against the all-out assault. In 1645, after the formation of the New Model Army, Fairfax was to storm Bridgewater with total success after only a week's delay, despite it being one of the most strongly-fortified towns in England, and against the advice of all his officers and advisers. Less than two months later he was to storm Bristol after only six days delay, and

A rather formidable portrait of Countess Derby in later life. It was said that she had 'stolen the Earl's breeches' by defending Lathom House in her husband's absence. [National Portrait Gallery.]

Lord Strange, later 7th Earl of Derby. [National Portrait Gallery.]

This nineteenth-century engraving presents a much pleasanter image of Charlotte, shown here with her husband Lord Derby and their daughter. [By permission of E. Winder.]

A portrait of the dashing German General, Prince Rupert of the Rhine.
[National Portrait Gallery.]

secure Prince Rupert's surrender after little more than two hours' fighting. Since the assault was so much a part of the man's military philosophy, it seems strange that he did not advocate it at Lathom. It may be that Fairfax was inhibited by a chivalric disinclination to make war on a woman. Or it may well be true that his later preference for storm over siege was a reaction against his experiences at Lathom.

Whether or not Fairfax was for a drawn-out siege, it was, in fact, that strategy which emerged from the council of war, as is outlined by Seacome and confirmed by the diarist from statements made by prisoners taken on the 12th.

The decision to go for an all-out siege was influenced by a rather strange conversation and set of circumstances, which are only reported by Seacome. It is such a strange story, unsubstantiated by the diarist, that we might be disinclined to believe it, except that circumstantial evidence, in the form of otherwise inexplicable behaviour by the besiegers would seem to support it. According to Seacome this story involved 'a captain of the parliament party there before the house during the time of treaty with the Lady; observing one of her Ladyship's chaplains . . . (the two men) had received their education together and were not only well-acquainted – but intimate and familiar with each other'.

The chaplain was undoubtedly Samuel Rutter while the parliamentary captain was very probably Captain Ashurst, from Ashurst Hall in Dalton, less than two miles from Lathom House.

> . . . At the close of the before-mentioned parley with the Lady, the Captain, getting an opportunity for free discourse with the afore-said Chaplain, attempted . . . to gain from him the secrets of that council by which the Lady had resolved to keep the house and asked of him, by virtue of their old friendship, to tell him truly upon what confidence she proceeded to reject the offers made her by the Parliament, to think to defend her house against so great a strength as was then before it encamped in the park.

Here Rutter, by accident or design, with or without the promptings of Lady Derby, resolved upon a bluff that could well avert the serious threat to the house. As one of Lady Derby's advisers, he was very well aware of the strengths of the house in the extent of its provision, and just as well aware of its weaknesses in the small size of the garrison together with the shortage of arms and ammunition. Lathom House could well survive any attempt to starve it into submission where it was not in a position to withstand an all-out attack. Rutter, therefore, when he answered his old friend, inverted the truth.

Indicating the numbers of soldiers and cannon on view, (which places this meeting on the Saturday when Rigby and Assheton went to the house together) Rutter stated that Lady Charlotte would welcome an attack as she knew that the numbers, and courage, of her soldiers were more than enough to repel such an attack. But, 'the Lady had but little provision of victuals in the house . . . that she would not be able to subsist above fourteen days for want of bread to supply the number of her soldiers . . . and she must inevitably be forced to surrender the place'.

At the council of the parliamentary leaders on the 5th or 6th of March, this captain (Ashurst or whoever) repeated what he had learned from Rutter. The significance of what he had to say was obvious. If the besiegers could keep up a close ward on the house so as to prevent supplies from reaching the garrison, the house would be forced to give way within two weeks, and surrender out of starvation.

It was an overwhelming argument in favour of siege whatever might have been Fairfax's opinion. For him it was academic anyway. He had received the recall he had wanted, and been relieved of the command of the siege at Lathom. He could now go back to Yorkshire, and initiate the process that would ultimately lead to the triumph of parliament in the North. Implementation of any plan for the investment of Lathom was to be left to Peter Egerton.

———————————

Chapter Seven

March 6 – April 1, 1644
Egerton in command —
The siege intensifies

ETWEEN Wednesday, March 6, and Saturday, March 9, teams of local people were conscripted in order to begin the process of digging those trenches and earthworks that would ultimately surround the house. This was the first move under the new regime, the physical isolation of the house being a necessary preliminary to cutting off the garrison's food supplies and channels of communication. The diggers may have included soldiers from the parliamentarian army, but the majority seem to have been farm labourers and smallholders from the Ormskirk area, impressed at gun-point if necessary for the work.

The focal point of the besiegers' earthworks, their forward base, was located, according to the diarist, 'in a stooping declining ground' so that the workers would be protected by the lie of the land from any gunfire from the house. The most probable site for this is where the remains of earthworks have recently been discovered, near to the headwaters of the Spa brook, the valley of which could be used for comings and goings between the forward position and the main camp in the Tawd Valley, while concealing these comings and goings from the marksmen on the walls of the house.

Away from the siege, the defenders were not entirely forgotten. By this time Lord Derby had returned from the Isle of Man to assist Byron in Chester. On Thursday, March 7th, he had written to Prince Rupert from Chester, asking for the prince's help in raising the siege. He no doubt pleaded for help on the basis of blood-ties and friendship, but Prince Rupert also had the military responsibility. In early February the king had appointed his nephew President of Wales and the Marches, with additional responsibility for the whole of north-western England, including Lancashire. On February 19th the prince had transferred his headquarters to Shrewsbury. Despite the urgency, and personal nature, of Derby's request, Prince Rupert had other, more urgent concerns in early March. Even as Lord Derby's letter reached him he was preparing to march to the relief of Newark which was under siege by Meldrum; Rupert left Shrewsbury for the east on Friday, March the 15th. Derby and Byron were entrusted with keeping Cheshire and Shropshire loyal to the king while Rupert was absent. Perhaps something might be done for Lathom at some future date, but for the moment it was not a priority in Rupert's eyes and the house's garrison would have to fend for themselves.

On Sunday, March 10th, there was an unexpected intervention in the siege. A delegation of six men, of some standing in the area, came to the house under a flag of truce to present a petition to Lady Charlotte, a petition which essentially begged her to accept the favourable terms Fairfax had offered. In this way some measure of peace could be restored to a countryside that was suffering from the depredations of both sides:

> That, in duty to her Ladyship, and love to their country, they most humbly beseech her to prevent her own personal dangers, and the impoverishing the whole country, which she might do, if she were pleased to slacken something of her severe resolution and in part condescended to the offers of the gentlemen.

The diarist, of course, represents this delegation as yet another ploy on the part of the parliamentarians, claiming that the six local men were told what to say and rehearsed in their lines, 'having thrust a form into their hands, and prepared their heads with instructions.' It may well be that that was the case, but we should not forget that to the people living in the vicinity of Lathom House, who were attempting to carry on with their normal existence, there was much cause for complaint. It has been estimated that much less than half the population of England were ever actively involved in the civil wars, on either side. For the majority, who were not involved, who were trying to lead a normal life despite the chaos around them, there must have been a mood of 'a plague on both their houses' as the tide of war washed across the comfort of their lives.

Let us consider the position of people living in the Ormskirk area. Between May 1643 and February 1644, they had had to put up with demands from Lady Derby for support and supplies. The 'nest of brigands' description given to Lathom House by Rigby in this period probably refers to requests for 'voluntary contributions' made by Lady Derby's representatives, with the backing of a body of armed men. At the same time as they were meeting these 'requests' the district also had to support the soldiers billeted upon them by Rigby, who, no doubt, not only demanded food and forage for themselves, but probably also imposed fines on those supplying Lady Derby, for 'trading with the enemy'. Since the end of February the district had also to face an army of 3,000 men who had been quartered on them, eating up their stores of food and forage, trampling down their crops and taking labourers off the land as forced labour.

In his book on the civil wars, John Kenyon describes some of the exactions made upon country districts by both sides. Chippenham, for example, in the period 1642-3, had to pay three taxes to parliament and two taxes to the king, as well as suffering a fine of £200 imposed by the royalists for dealing with the parliamentarians. Both parties did claim to pay for the costs of quartering soldiers on a district at the rate of 8d a day for troopers and 6d a day for foot soldiers. Mostly, these payments were on the basis of 'free quarter' which meant that no cash changed hands; food and forage being provided in return for promissory notes. These notes, however, were very seldom redeemed. The village of Wellow in Somerset was owed £1,202 10s 8d by the end of 1646, a sum that was never paid. The problem was so serious that, by 1645, many country districts were raising vigilante bands of 'club-men' to fight off intruding soldiers of either side. In the light of problems such as these, there was probably every justification for the men who went to Lady Derby with their petition, without their having to be prompted to do so by the parliamentarian forces.

Not that they had much joy from the Countess. What followed was a tribute to the great charm and persuasive power possessed by the lady, if she chose to exercise it. Lady Charlotte received them courteously and listened attentively to all they had to say. Then she outlined her version of the negotiations so far, summing up their various proposals and counter-proposals in such a way as to paint her own actions in the best possible light. This was done 'so smoothly and persuasively that the good men were satisfied and had little to say but, "God bless the King and the Earl of Derby"'. As if to twist the knife in the wound, Lady Derby sent the men away with a commendation to address their petition to the officers of parliament 'who are the real despoilers of the county.'

If the gentlemen had but known it, the Ormskirk area still had yet another twenty months of military operations to endure.

On Monday the eleventh, a new set of surrender proposals was taken to the house by John Ashurst, who is probably the captain who spoke to Rutter; he was certainly looked on with more favour than most of his colleagues, the diarist describing him as 'even and civil'. These new conditions began by waiving all previous proposals but then went on to repeat what had, substantially, been offered before. The Countess and all those with her would be free to go wherever they wished. There is no suggestion that arms had to be surrendered, although a parole would have to be given that they would not be used again against parliament. As to the time-scale, all bar a maximum of one hundred would have to leave the house at once, the remainder could have ten days grace.

There is an air of 'this is my final offer' about these proposals which were probably a token gesture by Egerton as the new commander to obey the convention which said that a call to surrender should precede any hostile action during a siege. The same convention accepted, as an inevitable consequence, that a defender would refuse the first demands, and would not surrender without at least one shot being fired. It was therefore no surprise to anyone when Lady Derby rejected these proposals as she had done those made earlier.

She replied that she refused to become a prisoner in her own house and reiterated her intention of preserving her honour and integrity by defending herself in arms. 'For what assurance do I have of liberty or good faith when my strength is gone?' She had every intention of defending the house against any attack, with God's help, and as a result declared her intention of receiving no more embassies or proposals. It was now known that Lord Derby had returned from the Isle of Man and it would therefore be better if any future proposals or demands were made directly to him.

Two weeks had passed by without a shot having been fired, nor any hostile or warlike act being committed by either side, except for the digging of trenches. On the day after Ashurst's abortive mission Lady Derby obviously decided to give the besiegers tangible proof that the time for talking was over. In the morning of Tuesday 12, a party of about one hundred foot soldiers, commanded by Major Farmer seconded by Lieutenant Brethergh of Childwall, issued out of the main gate. No shot was fired at them as they marched up to the line of trenches that were set between sixty and one hundred yards from the house. On the lip of the trench they halted and fired a volley into it, driving out the workers. As the besiegers clambered out of the trench and retreated, they were taken on the flank by Lieutenant Key, at the head of the house's cavalry, a total of twelve horse. In these actions Captain Ogle, with a small group of soldiers, covered the main gate during the attackers' absence, while Captain Rawsthorne did the same service at the postern gate by which the cavalry had left the house.

According to the diarist the besiegers lost thirty men, forty arms and six prisoners. There is no mention of any defensive action having been taken by those in the trenches so there is every possibility that this large number of casualties was due to their being mainly unarmed civilians pressed into service to dig the siege-works. Similarly, the large number of arms taken – presumably carbines and/or pikes – can be explained by the soldiers having stacked their arms while they worked in the trenches. As has been mentioned previously, the prisoners were interrogated, and it was from them that the garrison learned of the intention of the besiegers to starve them out.

Despite the success of that first attack, no further action was to be taken for the rest of the week. Indeed, although they were usually successful, the garrison made comparatively few such attacks. This is probably a confirmation of the garrison's desperate shortage of powder and shot, the bulk of supplies being kept for the gamekeepers and hunters who were employed as sharpshooters; men who could make every shot tell and who harassed the besiegers in their trenches. Nevertheless, even while conserving their gunpowder, the garrison noticed that their opponents were prone to take alarm during the night-watches. The next move made by the garrison, therefore, was intended to make the most of this nervousness in order to undermine the morale of the besiegers.

At three o'clock, in the early hours of Monday morning, a party of thirty musketeers, led by Captain Chisnall, with lieutenants Prethergh and Heape, silently made their way out of the postern gate at the rear of the house, intending to surprise the night watch in their trenches under cover of darkness. The glow from their slow-matches – the slow-burning fuses used by the musketeers to fire their muskets – betrayed the presence of the raiding party to the sentries. Having raised the alarm, the parliamentary soldiers ran away faster than their attackers could catch them and took refuge in the nearby woods. Being unwilling to risk his men among the trees, Chisnall returned to the house.

The fright occasioned by this night attack impressed the besiegers with the need to complete the encirclement of the house. Work on the trenches had been going on so slowly that the main ring-work had still not been completed and, more seriously, none of the siege-guns had yet been mounted. Now the parliamentarians were eager to bring up their cannon; if only to defend themselves from attack. The work to finish the trenches went on throughout Monday and Tuesday, with an increasing number of labourers impressed for the work, despite a constant sniping from the walls and towers of the house that resulted in a large number of civilian casualties. In an attempt to reduce these casualties the besiegers' engineers built a sort of testudo – a wooden framework on wheels that straddled the trench, roofed over with thick planks towards the house but open on the other side to allow earth to be cast out of the diggings.

The completed siege works consisted of three lines. The forward position was a deep, open trench, sixty yards from the house. The next line consisted of a ditch, three feet deep, on which were placed eight sconces, or temporary forts, each sconce defended, not only by a continuation of the ditch which surrounded each one, but by a rampart of beaten earth, six feet high. The ditch was sited one hundred yards from the house. Another hundred yards further back was the final ring consisting of a breast-work or earth wall.

.Over two weeks had passed since the council of war which had heard that the garrison only had food for two weeks. There must have been a growing suspicion in the parliamentarian ranks that something more than simple starvation was going to be needed to extricate the defenders of the house. The besieging forces lost no time now in bringing up their guns, the first cannon being mounted on the same Tuesday evening that saw the completion of the trenches. The first cannon to be mounted was their largest; a demi-cannon, together with a culverin, was mounted to the south-west of the house, facing the main gates. At a later date, after the mortar occupied the south-western battery, the big guns were moved to face the postern gate on the north-eastern side of the house. Nowhere does it say where the other two smaller cannon, both of them sakers firing five-pound balls, were mounted.

The demi-cannon was used for the first time on Wednesday the 20th, the day after it had been put in position. The first shot was aimed at the wall and made no impression at all. It may seem strange that walls that were almost two hundred years old could resist the impact of gunfire, yet their very age turned out to be their best defence. Where newer stone might have cracked or smashed under the impact, this old and weathered stone merely crumbled at the blow. The gunners soon realised that the wall was not going to collapse, and the other two shots fired that day were aimed deliberately high at the turrets and pinnacles surmounting the house. This gained no material advantage for them, but these more delicate structures did at least break most gratifyingly so as to give the impression that something was being done and, as the diarist says, 'to please the women that came to see the spectacle'. This reference is only the first of several which seem to indicate that the siege at Lathom was treated, especially during the Easter holidays, as some sort of free show for the people in the neighbourhood.

Once that initial bombardment was over the courtesies were resumed, with a letter sent into the house under flag of truce. The letter was in fact one received by Sir Thomas Fairfax from Lord Derby, and now he forwarded it to Lady Charlotte for her consideration. Lord Derby had written from Chester to ask Fairfax to intercede on behalf of his wife and children, asking that Lady Charlotte, with the children, should be given free passage from the house while leaving the garrison in place.

He was, he says, 'loathe to expose them to the uncertain hazards of a long siege, especially considering the roughness and inhumanity of the enemy, that joined pride and malice, ignorance and cruelty against her person'. Not exactly sentiments calculated to appeal to Fairfax, yet he passed on the letter to her ladyship, indicating that he was ready to re-open negotiations with her, bearing in mind that Derby had qualified his request with the statement, 'If it seems good to my wife.'

It is easy to guess at Lady Derby's consternation at this news. At no other time is it as clear that, far from being a helpless and persecuted woman, she was actually relishing the situation. She was acting the role of resolute defender and, she believed, doing so rather well. Now she could see it all being thrown away by Lord Derby, in ignorance of the circumstances, negotiating the surrender of the house when such a step was unnecessary.

For the moment she sought to gain time. She saw the messenger who had brought the letter to the house, 'one Jackson, a saucy and zealous chaplain to Mr Rigby', and entrusted the message to him that she would be quite willing to submit to her lord's commands, if those truly were his commands. She was equally willing that Lord Derby and Sir Thomas Fairfax should agree the matter between themselves. However, until it was absolutely certain that her husband really did want her to give up the house, 'she would neither yield the house nor herself desert it, but would wait for the event according to the good will of God.'

That night a messenger was got out of the house by the simple expedient of creating a diversion so that the messenger could escape into the darkness unseen by guards or sentries. The message was for Derby in Chester and, although we are not told what it said, it was no doubt intended to warn him off; informing him that Lady Derby was successfully resisting the besiegers and that matters could be safely left in her hands, with no need for any interference from him.

The relative ease with which a messenger was got out of the house, despite its supposed investment, suggests that the besiegers had nothing like as firm a grip on the garrison as might be supposed. Another reason for Lady Charlotte's intransigence could be that she was quite well informed as to the progress of the war elsewhere, and that it was going rather well for the king at that moment.

Even at that point in March the Scots' intervention had in effect come to nothing. Two months after their invasion of the North East, a combination of snow and Lord Newcastle's army had held up their forces at Chester-le-Street, short of Durham, while the city of Newcastle that they had been besieging since January had still not fallen. Meanwhile, Prince Rupert had marched from Shrewsbury to Newark, so relieving that town from Meldrum's siege. In what was virtually a rout, Meldrum had lost an incredible quantity of muskets and other small arms as well as thirty cannon, while many of his men had deserted to Rupert. With only 2,000 men Meldrum retired upon Hull to join up with Lord Fairfax. The relief of Newark had not only given Rupert a morale-boosting victory; it had secured the Midlands for the King and had placed the prince and his men athwart the Great North Road, separating parliament's strongholds in the South East from their allies in the North and Scotland.

To Derby this upturn in the King's fortunes meant some lessening of the pressure on Rupert, which in turn might mean that the Prince, as the king's Captain General for Lancashire, could turn his attention to the plight of Lathom House. James Stanley began to petition the King that Rupert might be given the mission of re-taking Lancashire for the King, relieving Lathom in the process. These pleas fell on deaf ears for the moment, but, if Lady Derby had any knowledge of these moves on her behalf, it no doubt strengthened her resolve to resist.

At Lathom no warlike activity is reported for the four days which followed Jackson's visit to the house with Derby's letter. But these days were very probably used to bring up the rest of the cannon and to establish the artillery batteries. Certainly the culverin, which could fire a fifteen-pound ball, was mounted alongside the demi-cannon by Monday March 25th. Both cannon were employed seven times that day, only one shot of which had any effect, though that was effective enough, one shot smashing through the main gate 'by some check in the way', which presumably means that the shot was a fluke ricochet. This success in breaking down the gate was not exploited and the damage was made good with a barricade of beds and furniture before anything could be done about it. It seems strange that, once having found a vulnerable point in the house's defences, the besiegers did not concentrate all their fire-power on the gates. The fact that they did not helps to reinforce the belief that the guns could not be aimed directly at the gates, and that the shot that broke them down was the chance outcome of a plunging shot or a deflected ricochet.

Once again there is an hiatus of two days, no action being mentioned by the diarist for Tuesday or Wednesday of that week. That is not to say that nothing did happen, since there are enough examples we know of that show the diarist was nothing if not selective in what he reported, and that he tended to ignore anything done by the besiegers that could not be shown in a discreditable or humorous light. Equally, of course, we have every reason to believe that the management of the siege was mishandled, and any failure on their part to exploit a temporary advantage cannot be regarded as unique.

On Thursday the cannon were in action again, five shots being aimed at the house. And then there follows another strange incident that cannot be explained. During the afternoon there were disturbances among the besiegers, as if they were fighting among themselves, and two shots from the cannon were discharged harmlessly into the air. In the journal this is dismissed as typical of the besiegers, whom the diarist stigmatises as being ever ready to panic, which seems to be too simple an answer but the only one we are ever likely to receive.

On the Friday there seems to have been a concentration of effort on the main gates. Reading between the lines of what the diarist says we can hypothesise that a plan was in existence to rush the gateway which would, of course, still be weakened by the events of Monday. The only explanation for the actions reported for that Friday was that efforts were made to pin down and neutralise the defenders on the wall, giving covering fire to any concentration of attackers. In the morning we are told that a marksman on one of the towers, who exposed too much of his body above the battlements, was 'shot to death'. The diarist is always specific when the cannon were involved, and the fact that they are not mentioned here suggests that this was an exchange of musketry between marksmen on both sides. During the afternoon, however, the cannon were employed, four shots being aimed specifically at those guns mounted on the gatehouse towers. In this action the garrison suffered its second fatality of the day when one cannon-ball, 'struck the battlements upon one of our marksmen, ready to discharge at the cannoneer, and crushed him to death.'

As I have said before, any attempt to interpret the motives of the besiegers purely from what the diarist says has to be pure speculation and cannot be supported. Nevertheless, I do believe that the exchange of gunfire that took place around the main gateway on the Friday, is best explained by a massing of parliamentarian soldiers outside the gate preparatory to an attempt at storming the house. Certainly, an abrupt change of strategy seems to have followed that Friday. By Sunday, the cannon had been re-mounted to face new targets, while, by the Tuesday, the mortar was occupying the battery opposite the main gates. As will be explained in the next chapter, we know from independent sources that dissension broke out in the parliamentarian ranks at about this time and that the main cause of this dispute was criticism over the handling of the siege. Again it is speculation but it is possible to believe that a strategy for exploiting the breaking down of the gates by a storming of the house had been evolved by one set of parliamentarian leaders, but was countermanded by others.

Whatever the explanation, two days of inactivity followed. On the Sunday night, there were two shots from cannon relocated so as to fire over the wall at the upper rooms of the house within. This was followed on Monday 1st April by a sporadic bombardment from cannon loaded with chain-shot and iron bars. Such ammunition was intended for use against people, rather than the fabric of the house, and its use can best be explained as an attempt to keep the defenders' heads down while the besiegers made fresh dispositions. On Tuesday those fresh dispositions were revealed by the first use of the mortar.

This giant mortar was lent by the leading Cheshire parliamentarian, Sir William Brereton. It was mounted some hundred yards to the southwest of the house, just beyond the ditch, where the land began to rise again, placed in a full-moon battery raised eight feet above the ditch so that the combination of rising ground and elevated position allowed the gunner a clear view of the fall of shot. On that first Tuesday it was used three times loaded with stone missiles thirteen inches across and weighing eighty pounds each. As yet these were simply shots aimed at finding the range.

Chapter Eight

April 2 – April 20, 1644
Rifts appear in the ranks

T about this time a serious rift developed between the leaders of the besieging forces. Although we have no precise details, there is overwhelming circumstancial evidence of a divisive split between the parliamentarian commanders that left the unity of their cause irreparably damaged. The division was essentially between Egerton and Rigby on the one side and Assheton and Moore on the other. At some time during the last week of March, Assheton and Moore removed themselves from the immediate vicinity of Lathom House, taking up quarters in Ormskirk, before withdrawing completely from any part in the siege. Before departing they took the unusual step of issuing an open letter that can, in one sense, be read as an implied criticism of the current leadership:

To all Ministers and Parsons in Lancashire, well-wishers to our success against Lathom House, these –
Forasmuch as more than ordinary obstructions have, from the beginning of this present service against Lathom House, interposed our proceedings, and yet still remain, which cannot otherwise be removed nor our success furthered, but only by divine assistance, it is thus our desires to the ministers and other well-affected persons of this county of Lancaster, in public manner, as they shall please, to commend our case to God, so the Almighty would crown our weak endeavour with speedy success in the said design.
Ralph Assheton,
John Moore,
Ormskirk, Apr. 5, 1644.

This letter was an object of ridicule as far as the diarist was concerned, who represented the two colonels as canting hypocrites. An element of religious self-righteousness there no doubt was; Lady Derby was not above invoking the deity on her own behalf. But there seems to be more to it than that. If we summarise the sentiments of the letter and put it into twentieth-century vernacular, it could well be that what the two colonels were saying was, 'God help us because no one else can'.

There was, of course, rather more to the disagreement than simple frustration at the course of the siege, as might be seen from a letter written by Ralph Assheton over a year later. At that time Assheton's son was serving in the army during the second siege of Lathom House, and Assheton's name was being put forward as the possible commander of the siege. From a letter written by Assheton to a fellow parliamentarian officer we get, not only his reaction to this suggestion, but also an indication of the depth of his antagonism towards Egerton and Rigby:

2nd July, 1645.

Mr Norris,

I rejoice to hear that my son's regiment does so well before Lathom, as is represented in your letter. You seem much to desire my coming down, but I see few others desirous of it and here it is represented that it is Col. Holland and Col. Rigby who are the men desired by the county. If it be so you shall not have me come amongst you, for *I will never join with them again.* Nevertheless I will here do the best service I can for my county so that you do show such respect to my son and his officers and soldiers as may encourage him to continue in your service. But if Stanley, Booth, Holcroft, Egerton, and such like must be applauded I will not only stay here, but send for my son to come to me for *I scorn that he shall receive orders from them.*

The letter thus far sings with the depth of Assheton's contempt for the leading group of Lancashire parliamentarians. He refuses to have anything further to do with Holland or Rigby, and he feels so strongly about a list of names including Egerton and Booth that he cannot even bear to have his son serve under them. Whatever caused the quarrel in the course of the first siege, it must have bitten very deeply to have so divided the man who was the military leader of the county from the men who had the political direction of the struggle. Part of the disagreement must have arisen from contempt for the military qualities of Holland, Rigby and Egerton; a contempt that was confirmed by the devastatingly withering scorn poured upon Holland and the other Manchester leaders by Johann Rosworm in his legal action after the war was over. Assheton, however, was not only questioning the ability of the Manchester committeemen, but also their moral probity and the legal shortcomings of their actions. In the second half of the same letter he continues:

I am much displeased at the committal of Col. Birch and Mr Harrison because I know they are honester and have done more faithful services for the Parliament than all those others which did commit them. I hear the principal complaint against Col. Birch was his opposing the great lay for the leaguer of Lathom, in which matter he did so well so much service for the country (for it was illegal both in matter and in manner) that I much wonder that the county does not petition Parliament for the release of him and the committal of all of them.

The point over which Assheton (and presumably Moore) differed with Rigby and Egerton was therefore the heavy tax levied on Lancashire to help pay for the siege. Significantly, the possibility of this tax was first mooted in late March, at the very time that the disagreement between the parliamentarian colonels first came to the surface. The total sum involved was £4,627 6s 4d, assessed on the whole county, with the exception of Lonsdale Hundred, and was, moreover, almost precisely the same sum as was raised by the then Lord Strange during the Bishops War. One can see Assheton's point: if that tax raised by Stanley was so illegal as to provoke Rigby to have him impeached in parliament, what now made Rigby's actions so very different, or any more legal?

Assheton no doubt followed Fairfax in seeing the siege of Lathom as an irrelevance, a distraction from the true purpose of the war, and as wasteful of men and resources, when Lady Derby with her garrison posed no more of a threat than could be contained by a watch such as the one that had been maintained before February. The purpose of the tax was said to be for the payment of extra soldiers. What need was there for extra soldiers when the besiegers already outnumbered the garrison by ten to one? There was also the dubious legality of raising the tax on all hundreds when only the Hundred of West Derby was directly involved.

Despite Assheton's reservations, and the more vocal objections of men such as Birch, the tax assessment on the county was passed. It did, however, meet with so many delays and excuses for non-payment that the committee was forced to meet again in late April, the tax demand being re-issued more forcefully on April 23rd, with penalties imposed for late payers and defaulters. Very little of the tax was ever paid.

In the meantime, the siege went on with only Egerton and Rigby left of the original commanders.

AFTER the initial firings of the mortar there was a day's delay in which, presumably, the gunnery officer made his finer calculations and the battery in which the mortar was sited was made more secure. Then, on Thursday the 4th, the mortar again fired a ranging shot with stone, followed immediately by the first grenade. Whether the gunner had not allowed for the lesser weight of the grenade compared to the stone is not known, but this first grenade completely overshot the house. The garrison had taken note of the threat posed by the mortar loaded with grenade and had prepared counter-measures which included men on fire watch with untanned and dampened hides to put out any flames.

The threat of the mortar was very real. As we have seen, the lie of the land prevented the besiegers' cannon from being depressed sufficiently for them to play on the base of the wall. Even if the ground had been such as to allow it, it is doubtful that anything less than a full-size cannon throwing a fifty pound ball would have the power to penetrate a wall thirty feet high and six feet thick. And the largest gun in the besiegers' hands was a demi-cannon with, as the name suggests, only half of the power required. Some engineering work was begun in a bid either to undermine the wall, or to divert the house's water-supplies. But all such bids were unsuccessful, making it quite clear that there was no way that the walls were going to be breached. The mortar, on the other hand, could throw its missiles in a high trajectory over the wall, directly into the house. Among the missiles that could be thrown like this were incendiary devices such as burning pitch, or grenades which were explosives packed into a fragmenting shell-case. Secure enough against the cannon, behind their stout stone wall, the garrison in fact were housed in a much weaker structure. As the diarist says, 'The house, though well fenced against the shot of cannon, has much inward building of wood, an ancient and weak fabric, with which many men's lives were nakedly exposed to the mortar'. Until now the garrison had almost been laughing at the besiegers, daring them to do their worst. Despite the besiegers having more men, more guns and more ammunition, the garrison knew that they were unassailable behind their walls. Faced with the mortar, however, the walls, instead of being a defence, became a trap for the garrison.

For some reason, nowhere explained, the besiegers made no immediate attempt to capitalise on their advantage. After the ineffectual shot of April 4th, no mention is made of the mortar until the 12th. Why this was the case, when the house lay defenceless before the mortar, we do not know. It could be that there were attacks unreported by the diarist, but, on the whole, he was more likely to exaggerate any aggression against the house rather than minimise it. A more likely explanation is that the besiegers were short of the grenades they needed for a steady and sustained bombardment of the house. Perhaps one of the objects of the Lancashire tax was to pay for supplies of the grenades.

As it was, after almost a week of inaction, it was the garrison who took the initiative, with an all-out attack on Monday, the 10th.

At eleven o'clock in the morning, a force of one hundred and forty men, commanded by captains Farmer and Molyneux-Ratcliffe, seconded by lieutenants Penketh and Worrall, left the house by the postern gate on the north-eastern side of the house. Captain Chisnall was left to guard this gateway with the reserve, while a similar guard was mounted on the main gates under the command of Captain Ogle. Captain Rawsthorne was on the top of the gatehouse towers from where his marksmen-snipers could best harass the enemy. Co-ordinating the attack was Captain Foxe from the top of the Eagle Tower, where he had a bird's eye view of the whole action and could direct the proceedings by the use of signal flags.

The main force got out of the house without difficulty. The sally port to the north-east was much used by the garrison because, although a gun battery was mounted opposite the gate, the downward slope of the ground towards the Tawd at this point meant that the cannon could not be depressed sufficiently to bear on those leaving the house. The men with Farmer and Ratcliffe were therefore able to walk right up to the guns while remaining under the line of fire, thus driving out the gunners without meeting opposition. Having secured the battery, they set some of their men to nail up the guns, while the remainder embarked on their immediate objective which was to clear the besiegers from their trenches and, in particular, from the sconces on the trenches. Their strategy seems to have been to divide the party so that one group went through the trenches like ferrets, flushing out the soldiers, while a second group drove off the soldiers as they emerged.

Two men are singled out for mention by the diarist. Ratcliffe, we are told, supported by just three soldiers, cleared two of the sconces personally killing seven men in doing so. Lieutenant Worrall, as his second-in-command, having captured one of the sconces was then himself attacked by fifty of the besiegers, but succeeded in holding them off until Farmer came up to relieve him. To everyone's surprise, according to the diarist, Worrall emerged from this encounter without a scratch. Indeed, if the diarist is to be believed, the attackers came off very lightly, with only one man killed, although the number of wounded is not given. Against this, again according to the diarist, the besiegers lost fifty men, sixty pieces of small-arms, one flag and three drums. A sour note is introduced when the diarist almost casually mentions in passing that a 'no prisoners' policy has been adopted by the garrison. It is claimed that an exchange of prisoners was agreed by Assheton and Rigby in their discussions with Lady Charlotte but that, although the garrison had released their prisoners, there had been no corresponding release of royalists held in Lancaster and Preston as had been agreed. Being unable to keep prisoners in the house, and having no faith in an exchange agreement, the garrison now proposed to give no quarter. In this attack just one officer was taken prisoner for the sake of the intelligence he could give them.

Having secured the trenches, the attackers proceeded to nail up all the cannon. They attempted to deal with the mortar in the same way but its mouth was too wide for them, and they had to content themselves in over-turning the weapon and trying to hammer the bore out of true. All their objectives having been achieved, the attacking force re-grouped and, rather than return through the postern gate, marched in triumphal display around the house to enter through the main gates, their passage being covered by Ogle and his musketeers.

However much the achievements of the attackers were exaggerated by the diarist, there is no gainsaying the extent of their success; even if it is only measured in terms of its effect on morale – positive for the garrison and negative for the besiegers. Although one saker fired twice before dark to prove that not all the cannon had been spiked, a state of alarmed agitation remained with the besiegers all night, with 'nothing but shouts and cries, as if the cavaliers had still been upon them'. One effect of this attack, according to Seacome, was a renewed call for a change of leadership and policy in the conduct of the siege on the part of the parliamentarians. In Rutter's version of events, as quoted by Seacome, Rigby took the opportunity created by the defeat of April 10 to accuse Egerton before the Manchester Committee of neglect and dilatoriness in prosecuting the siege, and of being personally responsible for the defeat. Rigby's complaint was successful in having Egerton removed from the command, Rigby himself being appointed as his successor.

It is one possible explanation for Rigby's promotion but, as is so often the case with Seacome's account, it is doubtful at best. Both of the two men, Rigby and Egerton, worked harmoniously together later and there is no hint of the estrangement one might have expected if such a charge had been laid by Rigby against the Salford colonel. The reason given by parliament for the change was that Egerton was needed by the Manchester Committee so that he could take part in the renewed debate on the tax to be levied, a debate due to take place on April 23. Indeed it is on that date, the 23rd, that the diarist first mentions Rigby as being in command of the siege.

Whether there was a change of command at this point, or whether it was merely that the attack of the 10th galvanised the besiegers into a more positive frame of mind, it is clear that the next few days saw the start of a crescendo of violence leading up to the climactic moment of the siege.

On Friday the 12th the mortar was fired twice, without any reported success, but sufficient to show that the weapon the garrison had most cause to fear was still in action. On the same day a chance shot from a saker in the north-eastern battery happened to penetrate the window of Lady Charlotte's bedchamber but the shot had lost its momentum and, 'was too weak to fright her from her lodging.' By the next day one of the demi-cannon had been unspiked and was fired. This shot was very weak, however, since the gunners suspected that the gun might have been 'poisoned', which is to say that an extra charge of powder might have been hidden in the body of the gun so that, if it were shotted normally the excess powder would cause the cannon to explode.

The intensive campaign began on Monday, April 15th. The mortar was fired six times; five times loaded with stone, but with a grenade for the sixth. This proved to be the most devastating blow yet. The bomb fell within the house, dropping onto a walk between the walls and the Chapel Tower. Shrapnel fragments from the exploding shell-case were two inches thick, and were scattered over the whole area of the house, and over the walls, by the force of the blast.

On the following day, Tuesday, the besiegers kept up the pressure. They began the morning with a double bombardment from the now unspiked cannon, and followed it with half an hour's musket-play. At eleven the mortar was used with a stone ranging-shot. Seeing that the stone fell into the very heart of the house the gunner immediately followed it up with a grenade fired on the same trajectory. The missile fell into an old courtyard within the older part of the house, digging a crater for itself nearly two feet deep but then rising again and bursting in mid-air. The blast was tremendous: 'it shook down the glass, clay and the weaker buildings near it, leaving only the carcase of the walls standing.' Two women in a nearby room had their hands burned, presumably in staunching fires started by the blast.

The psychological effect of the mortar was just as important as its destructive impact and, although no actual action is reported for the rest of that week until Saturday, it is as though the besiegers deliberately left the garrison in suspense to let their fears of the mortar prey upon their minds. The walls no longer provided a refuge against the enemy without, but had become instead the bars of a cage, pinning them down as sitting targets within lath and plaster walls that would disintegrate in an explosion and surrounded by timber that would burn. It is at this point that the rank-and-file soldiers mutinied, refusing to sleep in the upper rooms with their flimsy plaster walls unless the officers left their ground floor, stone-walled rooms so as to share in their men's accommodation.

Repeatedly the diarist speaks of the fears felt by the garrison in respect of the mortar: 'The mortar-piece was that that troubled us all. The little ladies had stomach to digest cannon, but the stoutest soldiers had no heart for grenades', 'Their grand terror was the mortar-piece which had frighted them from meat and sleep.' In the atmosphere of fear that must have pervaded the house one can only assume that the sombre religious celebrations of Holy Week must have taken on an added solemnity as the garrison waited for the next blow to fall.

Just one incident relieved the all-pervasive gloom. On the Tuesday during the firing of the mortar, one of Morgan's gunners, climbing up onto the rampart surrounding the mortar so as to see the fall of shot, was hit and killed by a sniper's shot from one of the towers. A minor triumph, but all-important, when the possibility of defeat was all too real.

Meanwhile, in the war at large a train of events was set in motion that was to lead temporarily to the relief of Lathom but ultimately to its destruction.

Since January the situation east of the Pennines had been a stalemate.

The king's Army of the North under Lord Newcastle had been divided, with half – under Newcastle himself – based in Durham to face the Scots and prevent their progress southwards; and half, under John Belasyse, based at Selby keeping Lord Fairfax bottled up in Hull. Late in March, the stalemate was broken by Belasyse making the decision to attack Lambert, returning from Lancashire by way of Bradford. With the royalist commander's attention thus distracted, Sir Thomas Fairfax had the chance to slip past to join Lord Fairfax, who came out of Hull just as soon as Belasyse's back was turned. Father and son joined forces at Ferrybridge. There they were joined by Lambert, fresh from success at Bradford, and by Meldrum, with the men he had rescued from the defeat at Newark. Together the men commanded a force of around 6,000 men, an army almost as strong as the 6,500 men led by Belasyse who had now returned to his headquarters in Selby.

The instructions to Meldrum and the Fairfaxes from the Committee of Both Kingdoms in London was that they were to march north to join forces with the Scots. They chose to ignore the instruction and, on 11th April, the very same day as the successful attack by the Lathom garrison, the parliamentary Yorkshire Army attacked Selby. The result of a day's bitter fighting through the streets of the town, was the virtual destruction of Belasyse's army and the capture of Belasyse himself.

Lord Newcastle received the news the next day and had no alternative but to break off contact with the Scots, and race for York, before the northern capital was lost. Newcastle entered York on April 15th, sending away Goring with the Northern Horse so that the cavalry should not be pinned down if the city were besieged. Leven and the Scots, in slow pursuit of Newcastle, joined the Fairfaxes, outside Tadcaster, on Saturday, April 20th. Sir Thomas Fairfax detached Meldrum from the new joint command. His brief was to shadow Goring and to give any advance warning of an attempt to relieve York from the west. Then the allied armies moved to begin the siege of York on April 22nd – Easter Monday.

The threat to York was the catalyst which re-awakened the king and Prince Rupert to a concern for the plight of the North, a concern that took into consideration the fate of Lathom House.

Chapter Nine

April 20 – May 25, 1644
Rigby in command
Climax and anti-climax

HE short but successful mortar barrage of April 16th was followed by a brief lull. The religious probity of both sides probably ensured an absence of any military action on Maundy Thursday and Good Friday. On the parliamentarian side there was probably an additional reason for an hiatus in the besieger's activities. This was the most probable date for the recall of Egerton and the appointment of Rigby as commander of the siege. We know that Egerton had to be in Manchester for the 23rd, while the intensity of the action during the week which began on that Saturday, the 20th, bears all the hallmarks of Rigby's passionate hatred for the House of Stanley.

During the Saturday morning the demi-cannon and the culverin, sited in the north-eastern battery opposite the postern-gate sally port, were employed no fewer than thirty times, in an attempt to breach the walls at this point. There was a logic in their action since this postern-tower projected beyond the moat without the defences of the main gates and therefore offered the best chance for entering the house through a breach in the walls. Unfortunately, they were defeated in their object by that same falling away of the ground we have mentioned earlier, so that, unable to depress the cannon sufficiently because of their location on an up-slope, all the shots were aimed too high and caused very little damage beyond the destruction of some battlements and the removal of about a yard of wall; damage which, according to the diarist, was made good the same night.

In the afternoon the besiegers abandoned their cannon in favour of the far more formidable mortar, employing it five times. The diarist makes no mention of the outcome of these attacks but, since he is very quick normally to sneer at the besiegers' failures, and he does not do so on this occasion, we must assume that the five shots were at least successful in damaging the morale, if not the fabric, of the house and garrison. Emboldened, the besiegers attempted a night action, firing the mortar three times after dark, twice using stones and once with a grenade. The gunner, however, was less confident of his aim at night and the grenade that was meant to be the finishing touch fell short of the house.

The unofficial truce that seemed to prevent military action on the part of either side every Sunday, applied now with even more force, and Easter Day itself passed without incident. Easter Monday on the other hand was a wakes holiday for the county that carried no such religious inhibitions. Once again many local people regarded the siege as a free show, a good excuse for a day out and picnic – with entertainment laid on. Large crowds of spectators had turned up on this Monday, to see and cheer anything Rigby might do for their amusement. Here, too, we see that Rigby understood the benefit of good public relations. The crowd was treated to half an hour of musket-fire, followed by the cannon firing nine times and the mortar, loaded with stone, twice. The crowd cheered and shouted for every hit. There was little or no damage to the house but the show was impressive.

The Tuesday was also a holiday and even more spectators were there to see the fun. Rigby did not disappoint them, having dreamed up an even more spectacular show. The guns in the north-eastern battery, the demi-cannon and the culverin, were normally aimed too high for the missiles to have any effect on the walls. Now that natural elevation was used deliberately, to bring the cannon to bear on the Eagle Tower. Someone with knowledge of the house had obviously briefed the gunners as to where the wall of the tower was weakest through having a staircase running up within it. A constant pounding of a small area of wall had its effect when the staircase was opened up, creating a large breach through which the gunners put several more shots, two of which actually penetrated Lady Charlotte's bedchamber.

There was very little gain in military terms from this bombardment, although Lady Derby had to look for a new bedroom while repeating that she would 'keep the house while there is a roof to cover her head'. On the other side, two gunners were killed, shot by marksmen located on the very tower at which they were aiming. However, Rigby had more than a military motive in what he had done. He was well aware that those same spectators that he was trying to impress were also tax-payers who were being asked to pay for the siege. It was in his interests to see that the spectators felt that they were getting their money's worth.

It was at this point that Rigby was tempted into giving a hostage to fortune by making a rash commitment. Acknowledging the fact that he had given the spectators good sport, he went on to invite them to come back on Friday to see something even better; he promised to level Lathom House to the ground on the afternoon of that day. Not content with a potential audience made up of purely local notables, he went on to extend the invitation to the Manchester Committee, and all the more important dignitaries of the county. Having been given command of the siege he intended to bring about a speedy and successful end to it and wanted as large and as influential an audience as possible while doing so.

In the meantime the garrison had discovered a new game with which to torment the besiegers. On Monday night two musketeers carrying matchlocks had sneaked out of the house after dark, in an attempt at making a surprise attack. They had been discovered and the besiegers had set off their mortar, two of the cannon and a hail of musket-fire in a bid to repel the supposed attack. The two musketeers were unharmed; merely amused at the stir they had created, which was surely an over-reaction to the threat posed by just two men. The garrison considered how they could best provoke a similar panic, and decided that this whole affair had been sparked off by the sentries in the trenches sighting the glow of the musketeers' slow-matches.

On Tuesday night the besiegers again saw the twin glow of two slow matches. The alarm was given and the cannon discharged, only to find that the cause of the alarm was two lengths of slow-match that had been fixed into balls of clay and thrown out of the house. It was a trick the garrison found amusing and it was one they were to repeat, in ever more elaborate variations, through the weeks to come. It was a device that never failed to cause panic among the besiegers, with consequent confusion and embarrassment when the truth was known.

By Wednesday the spectators had gone. Rigby contented himself with the mortar played three times, using stone, and two shots from the guns. On the other hand, a full supply of grenades had been received and a possible resolution of the siege seemed imminent.

On the Thursday a messenger went to the house with what Rigby describes as his 'last and final offer'. There were no concessions, nor any negotiating positions, in what he had to say. The message simply stated that she must surrender the house, together with all the people, goods and armaments, throwing herself on the mercy of parliament. All this to be agreed before two of the following afternoon. The proposed course of action, if she refused, was to be the use of the mortar so as to burn the house down around her ears.

Lady Charlotte's defiance of this ultimatum permitted her to make the most histrionic of her speeches, in a set-piece theatrical setting that caught the popular imagination, so that a romanticised picture of the scene, by a painter from a more sentimental period, still hangs in Knowsley House. Having read Rigby's letter she called for the messenger and told him that he deserved to be hung from the gatehouse towers for bringing such a message, and should have been if he had been more than a dupe and mouthpiece for the real author of the ultimatum. Then she tore the paper across, in a dramatic gesture of defiance, and went on, 'Tell that insolent rebel, he shall have neither persons, goods or house. When our strength and provision is spent, we shall find a fire more merciful than Rigby and then, if the providence of God prevent it not, my goods and house shall burn in his sight. Myself, my children and my soldiers, rather than fall into his hands, will seal our religion and loyalty in the same flame'. We are told that all those of the soldiers who heard her reply broke out in cheers at her defiance, and swore to die alongside her rather than give Rigby any satisfaction.

The proud sound of defiance was very well in the heat of the moment but one second's reflection must have told them of the seriousness of their situation. The events of the past few weeks had told them of the havoc that could be wrought by just an occasional grenade falling into the enclosure. Now they faced the prospect of a sustained bombardment by the same weapon. There was no defence against the fall of the grenades beyond the ability of snipers to harass the gunners working the mortar; and that could only postpone matters, not prevent them. For all their gallant defiance the garrison was faced with the simple choice of either staying where they were to await the inevitable, or of staking everything on one last, desperate venture. As the diarist says, it had become a question of 'kill or be killed'. An attack was planned that would involve virtually the entire garrison in one capacity or another.

The garrison was roused before dawn at four o'clock and went to their allotted stations. Captains Ogle and Rawstorne kept the main and postern gates respectively, with small companies of guards. Ratcliffe took command of the marksmen and musketeers upon the walls and towers, while Captain Farmer maintained a reserve of fresh men in the central courtyard, ready to go to the relief of any of his colleagues in need. As it happens he was never called upon, and his men were later sent to augment the team of musketeers on the walls. All the soldiers remaining after these groups had been selected – the majority of the company – were divided into two companies and put under the command of captains Chisnall and Foxe, each of these captains seconded by two lieutenants.

At first light, Chisnall was the first to leave the house. His men left the postern gate and, keeping under the line of fire, gained the battery on which the demi-cannon was mounted, after a short skirmish. Having gained their foothold in the siege-works, Chisnall remained in the sconce he had captured, to secure the area commanding the postern. Foxe's company now took over, beating their way through the trenches, from that north-eastern battery to the battery opposite the main gates where the mortar was situated. This saw the fiercest fighting of the engagement, since there was a guard of fifty men around the mortar and they, being raised over ten feet above the ditch, proved very difficult to dislodge. At one point, unable to bring their muskets to bear, the men with Foxe were reduced to throwing stones at the defenders. After some fifteen minutes of hard fighting, however, Foxe and his men took the ditch and climbed the rampart, driving out the parliamentarians. Having gained the gun position, Foxe put a company of musketeers in to garrison it, thus thwarting the besiegers who had regrouped at a distance and attempted a counter-assault, which was beaten off by both the musketeers in the battery and the marksmen on the gatehouse.

With both major siege-works in their hands, the captains now had a total command of the trenches, in which they stationed their own men to cover the next stage in the proceedings. Protected by Captain Ogle, the servants of the house, led by Broome the steward, their numbers made up from those soldiers who had not been engaged in the fighting, left the house by the main gate and set to work in reducing the ramparts and in filling the ditch which surrounded the mortar emplacement. Once that had been done, the mortar was manhandled onto a low-loading wagon, or sled, and thus being made mobile was hauled into the house. Then, with Ogle covering the retreat, the soldiers withdrew in good order and the great gates closed on servants, soldiers and the mortar.

On Chisnall's withdrawal into the postern-gate, a similar attempt was made to capture the demi-cannon and culverin. Rawstorne serving in the same capacity as Ogle had done at the main gate. Here, however, a greater depth of ditch and the combined weight of the two cannon prevented them from having the same success. The besiegers, in making their counter-attack, were also assisted by not having to advance across open ground as was the case to the south west, but were able to mask their approach by coming up through the trees of the wooded Tawd Valley. In the face of these difficulties, and before being overwhelmed by superior forces, Rawstorne contented himself with nailing the cannon before he also retired into the house.

The whole action had lasted just one hour with the loss (according to the diarist) of only two men. It was, however, the turning point of the siege. The captured mortar, pulled into a courtyard of the house, became the focal point of wild celebrations. The mortar was likened to a 'dead lion' by the diarist, the men shouting and singing around it, taking it in turns to rest a foot on it in the gesture of a successful huntsman. The atmosphere was like a wedding feast or Christmas revels 'rejoicing as merrily as they used to do with their ale and bagpipes'. It was Lady Charlotte who calmed them by calling upon her chaplains to lead the assembled garrison in a service of thanksgiving.

More significantly, underlying the mood of celebration was a sense that the siege was essentially over. Never mind the besieging army and the remaining cannon; they had proved harmless in the past. Only the mortar could harm them and now that had been captured it was as though the main work was done and the rest was child's play.

If that were the mood within the house, it is not hard to guess at the atmosphere obtaining without the walls. For the besiegers in general, and Rigby in particular, it must rank as one of the great anti-climactic moments. Not only was there the defeat to contend with and the loss of the mortar, but Rigby also faced the shame of facing those members of the Manchester Committee who turned up at two o'clock that afternoon, at his invitation, to witness the culmination of the siege. For Rigby it was the end of his ambitions. Not only could he not deliver what he had promised, but he had, through his own actions, exposed himself to the ridicule of men who were not always his greatest admirers. The demonstration he had promised was supposed to be his justification for the huge tax levy imposed on Lancashire. In allowing the tax-payers of the county to witness the destruction of Lathom House he would, in effect, be saying, 'I know it was a lot of money but wasn't it worth it?' Now, with the mortar captured, the self-same tax-payers would be able to see that the money had, in fact, been squandered. There was no real prospect of them renewing the tax when it came up for renewal the following month.

Amid the ruin of his hopes, with his most powerful weapon gone, with the end of his funds in sight, and without support, Rigby had to recognise that there would be no easy end to the siege of Lathom House. There was nothing left but to begin again and return to the slow business of starving out the garrison.

If, in musical terms, the week leading up to the events of April 26th could be described as a crescendo, then the weeks that followed proved to be a long and dispiriting coda. The shock of losing the mortar and the embarrassing anti-climax of Friday, were followed by the withdrawal of all the cannon bar one, and that, for security, mounted too far off to be any threat to the house. During May it is difficult to tell who were the true besieged – those within or those without the house!

The one attempt made by the besiegers in this period was some work done by Browne, their engineer, in an attempt, either to tap into the house's water supply, or to drain the moat. Several ditches or tunnels were dug to this purpose but without success. This work was hindered greatly by fire from the marksmen on the walls; in the parliamentarian account of the siege it is said that the sluice dug to drain the moat ran, 'so near the House it was the death of many poor honest men'. It also did not help that the garrison knew all their plans for this work, having captured an assistant of Browne's during the action of April 26th, and learned all their intentions from him. In case the besiegers were intending to undermine the walls, a counter-mine was sunk from within the house.

There was so much digging of tunnels going on at this time that I wonder whether this might be the explanation for the holes and 'wells' that were found in the vicinity of the site, which were claimed at the time to be possibly part of the legendary secret tunnel Lathom House was supposed to possess. It is part of Ormskirk mythology that a tunnel ran from the house to a variety of possible destinations, of which Burscough Priory and Ormskirk parish church are the most remote. The fact that the diarist twice mentions messengers going in or out of the house, either by strategem or by shooting a sentry, would seem to preclude the existence of a more secret passage. The tunnelling done in May, together with the house's ability to withstand a close investment, probably combined in the popular imagination to create this legend of a secret passage. As it was, it was the weather that put an end to the engineering work. Never-ending rain in that spring finally turned the ground into a sloppy mud and the besiegers' tunnel collapsed, burying three miners alive.

The unseasonally heavy rain must have added considerably to the misery of those soldiers who had to man the trenches in the siege at Lathom. It is all too easy to see the effect it must have had on a morale already low as a result of the trauma engendered by the loss of the mortar. And it is true that morale sank ever lower as that May progressed. Obviously the diarist dwells lovingly on the panic and despair exhibited by the besiegers but then, as Miss Rice-Davies says, 'He would, wouldn't he?' A more objective view comes from the account of the anonymous author, who wrote a history of the war in Lancashire from the parliamentarian point of view, whose history was published by Beaumont in the last century. Considering the relevance of what he has to say about that May period of the siege, it is perhaps worth digressing for a moment and looking again at the siege from a standpoint different from that we have used so far.

The unknown author admits himself that he only wrote down his account two or three years after the war was over and it is therefore not very surprising if his memories are not always accurate; his dates are unreliable and he confuses the sequence of events. He places the start of the siege, for example, in late March and claims that the guns were only brought up and used after the mortar was taken; moreover locating the cannon battery to the north-west rather than the north-east of the house. Nevertheless, having acknowledged its faults, it is remarkable as to how often this account agrees, in detail, with the version given by the diarist.

The military action to secure the trenches is not mentioned but the capture of the mortar is reported, including the fact that it was loaded onto a sledge to be taken into the house. He is as positive as the diarist in describing the potential menace represented by the mortar, although claiming that only two grenades were ever fired. His description of the stone missiles hurled by the mortar is graphic. The stone 'would fly so high that almost a man could not see them and then the falling was so ponderous that they break down all where they lighted'. He mentions the destruction of a clock on the Chapel Tower so that its chimes were no longer heard by the besiegers; he does, however, claim that this was done by a stone missile, where the diarist says that the Chapel Tower was damaged by a grenade.

Although wrongly located in time, this account accurately describes the artillery bombardment of the Eagle Tower that the diarist assigns to Easter Tuesday. The cannon were used, 'against the Tower, playing vehemently against it one whole day, making a great breach in it that might easily be discerned'. The description of this bombardment, and the firing of the mortar, are sufficiently detailed as to suggest that the writer was an eye-witness, presumably as one of the spectators in the crowds that gathered during the Easter holidays.

Where this parliamentary account becomes most interesting, however, is when it is highly critical of the direction and intent of the siege and its leaders. Like the diarist he is amazed by the number of times that, just as the besiegers seem to be getting somewhere, that line of action is halted and no advantage is ever followed up. Of the mortar he says, 'if it had been applied to shooting as it might have been the house had been yielded up in a short while. . . it was feared by the Countess so much she did not know where to hide herself. . . if the besiegers had continued to shoot it but twice or thrice more, she had yielded up the House. But whereof it was not continued was not known to the soldiers'. And, again, of the bombardment of the Eagle Tower – '. . . and that was left off'. Even the engineering works came under suspicion, 'Browne the engineer was judged to be not so faithful as he might'.

The writer was therefore highly critical of the management of the siege and, like Assheton and others, especially critical of the cost and waste. 'It was a very costly siege to the county. There was needlessly spent on it shot and powder in infinite quantity. Some of them were always shooting at nothing they could see but the walls.' 'About twelve weeks the besiegers lay there with little or no effect but the loss of men's lives and spending of much treasure and victuals.'

The writer gives us some idea as to how the besieging forces were organised. Theoretically the various hundreds of the county were supposed to take turns in providing militia companies for the siege, but the writer only mentions detachments from Amounderness Hundred. This might be because the writer was a Kirkham man, and was only interested in those contingents who came from the Fylde. Or it may have been due to the fact of Rigby being colonel for Amounderness and, by the end of the siege, he had differed with so many of his colleagues that militia from all other hundreds had been withdrawn. Rigby himself appears to have been based permanently in Ormskirk, although he came to New Park House every day to consult with his captains. The officers and some of the men were billetted on the countryside 'in such houses as were able to receive them'. They were on duty 'every third day and night'.

All in all the diarist is no more critical of the bearing and conduct of the besiegers than is their own chronicler. Indeed, although he is highly critical of Lady Derby's obstinacy, he shows a lingering respect for Lord Derby and has a reluctant admiration for the skill of the garrison. Of the marksmen in particular he makes special mention of their technique of marking any loopholes in the besiegers works through which they could see, realising that when their view through the loophole was blocked it was probably because there was a man behind it and then having the skill to put a bullet through that hole, 'and thereby they killed many men'.

The picture that emerges of the condition of the besieging army after the seizure of the mortar is of men driven hard by unremitting duty, without real support from their leaders, ignorant as to the use and purpose of what they were doing but conscious of money and resources being wasted, and in constant fear of death. Is it any wonder if the parliamentary forces went to pieces in those weeks? This demoralisation was augmented and hastened by continued pinpricks from the men in the house, who '. . . gave many alarms in the night time to the guards, which was the occasion that much powder and shot was wasted'.

These night alarms were a continuation and elaboration of the game with the slow-match in the ball of clay, which the garrison had found so satisfying on the nights of the 22nd and 23rd April. Finding just how much alarm they could spread by the use of their clay-ball devices the garrison refined the trick into ever more bizarre forms. Matches were threaded into a long length of string that was twined through the trees near the house and them pulled so that a glowing snake seemed to move through the woods. Dogs were also set loose with lighted matches on their backs and an old horse starred with lighted matches like a constellation was set out to gallop through the besiegers' camp.

In the face of these constant threats and alarms, in the appalling weather conditions, in view of the futility of their actions, it might not be thought surprising that there was a sharp increase in desertion from the parliamentarian ranks. One deserter even attempted to join the garrison and even though his arrival was treated with suspicion by the Countess' advisers who suspected a trick, the defection worried Rigby to the extent of causing him to double the guard-duty. Rigby had good cause to fear one reason for desertion: the lack of pay. It was standard practice, in the armies of both sides, that foot soldiers were paid at the rate of six shillings a week, but the money was seldom forthcoming, being paid in arrears if at all. With the failure of the tax levy it is doubtful whether any money in sufficient quantities was available for the Lancashire forces. This might not have mattered if the soldiers had been assured of the eventual fall of the house, with the consequent possibilities of loot and plunder; but that eventuality seemed as far away as ever. Before he lost all his soldiers, with the trickle of deserters becoming a flood, Rigby was forced to pay part of the arrears of pay out of his own pocket. By the end of the siege he estimated that he had lost £2,000 of his own money.

To add to all his other problems it was at this time that Rigby's brother died and, on top of his troubles at Lathom, Alexander Rigby had to cope with his brother's funeral, the execution of his estate, which led to a succession of law suits, and with the guardianship of his two young children. No wonder that a note of despair crept into a letter Rigby wrote to the Manchester Committee in mid-May:

> We are obliged to repel them five or six times in one night. These constant alarms, the numbers of the garrison, and our great losses compel our men to mount guard every other night, and even two nights in succession. For my part I am spent in anxiety and fatigue.

On May 15th, Alexander Rigby was called to Manchester to account for the failure of the siege and also to help frame a response to a letter from the Earl of Denbigh who was in difficulties on the Welsh-Cheshire border and had appealed to Lancashire for assistance. In a reply dated May 16th, the Manchester Committee had to refuse such help -

> The siege of Lathom House continues not to be broken up, unless we will resolve to begin the whole work anew. The Earl of Derby in the Wirral and that part of Cheshire all along the river against us makes inroads upon us and keeps us in continued alarums. To break up the siege at Lathom would be no less than the hazard of the whole county.
>
> A. Rigby   R. Holland   R. Hyde   J. Holcroft
> T. Stanley   J. Booth   P. Egerton

On Monday, May 20th, Rigby returned to Lathom, bringing Holland with him, but the senior colonel had nothing new to suggest but to re-open negotiations. The two men drafted a letter together and, on Thursday, in the first communication with the house since the ultimatum of April 25th, Captain Edward Moseley was sent to hand this letter to Lady Derby.

There were no threats or warnings, indeed no possible sanctions that the besiegers could impose given the impotence they had shown over the intervening month. The letter was a straightforward demand that Lady Derby should surrender house, arms, possessions and people, and submit to the mercy of Parliament.

Lady Charlotte fully understood their impotence. We are told that she smiled as she read the letter, and responded by pointing out that there was a mistake in the wording which said 'mercy' instead of 'cruelty of Parliament' and when Moseley protested that 'mercy' was meant, went on, 'the mercies of the wicked are cruel. Not that I hold Parliament to be cruel, I hold it in esteem. But such agents as Rigby and Moore who submit the country to blood and ruin . . .'

Her defiance was greeted with rapturous applause, as always, but a new confidence upheld her audience in the support they gave her, since everyone was now aware of the weakness of the besiegers' situation. In fact, there was immediate proof of that weakness inasmuch as Moseley, having had the letter rejected, went on to say that if she wished she could have those exact terms that she had demanded from Fairfax at the start of the siege. If ever there was a signal that she had won, this was it. She merely replied that she was quite incapable of making such a major decision for herself and that the two colonels should contact Lord Derby and negotiate with him; for her part she merely awaited the orders of her husband.

That same evening she received the justification for her stand. A messenger got into the house, by shooting a solitary sentry who stood in his way. This man brought the news that Lord Derby was with Prince Rupert, and with a sizeable army, that they were on the march through Cheshire and were poised to enter Lancashire for the eventual relief of Lathom. The end, which had been inevitable since the taking of the mortar, was finally near to hand.

Chapter Ten

May 16 – May 28, 1644
Prince Rupert intervenes –
'The Yorke Marche'

N April 18th, just three days after he had arrived in York, Lord Newcastle wrote to the king about the imminent joining together of the Scots and Fairfax's army: 'they are now too strong for us in matters of the field. They have already put themselves in such a posture as will ruin us, being at York, unless there is some speedy course taken to give us relief'. What he did not know at that stage was that his position was even shakier than he suspected, since the allied army was to be joined in early May by the army of the Eastern Counties Association under the leadership of the Earl of Manchester, with, more significantly in the light of what was to happen, Manchester's relatively unknown leader of horse, Oliver Cromwell.

In the light of Newcastle's letter the king had to agree to Rupert making some attempt to relieve the situation in the North. But Charles was also very worried about the southern front and he insisted that he could not spare any of the troops in Oxford. Rupert would have to recruit his army en route. He therefore left Oxford on May 5th, with just his personal life-guard, under Sir Richard Crane, riding first to his base at Shrewsbury, where he collected the 2,000 horse and 6,000 foot he had used for the relief of Newark. He was also going to need Byron and Derby with the Cheshire army and here, in order to attract Derby's support, he promised to proceed by way of Lancashire, partly so as to gain Lancashire recruits, but also so as to relieve Lathom House.

Rupert left Shrewsbury on May 16th and marched to Knutsford where he was joined by Byron and Derby, their two armies making up the large total of 5,000 horse and 5,000 foot with a baggage train that included fifty-eight carriages. It was a force far in excess of the ability of any army then in Lancashire to resist them.

The royalist force also brought with it the supreme advantage of Rupert's reputation. Rupert's Horse had not been beaten or worsted in any battle or skirmish they had fought thus far. The very name of Rupert was enough to strike fear into his opponents, who were often ready to concede defeat before battle was joined. It is only unfortunate that Rupert's men did not live up to the high esteem in which their leader was held. They had gained an unenviable reputation for arrogance, indiscipline and indiscriminate cruelty. They were cavalrymen who thought of themselves as an elite and treated the infantry with such contempt that they would often disregard orders given by officers of foot regiments. Worse was their sheer inability to obey orders in battle; at Edge Hill, and later at Naseby, Rupert's cavalrymen won their first charge, breaking through the enemy ranks, only to keep on going in futile pursuit or looting, while behind them the balance of the battle turned against the king's side. One ultimately decisive factor was the discipline instilled into the parliamentarian cavalry by Cromwell and Fairfax so that, having broken the opposing line, they could turn and take the centre on the flank. However, at the time of his march to York these flaws were not yet apparent and the mere word of Rupert's approach was enough to clear his path of opposition.

Between Knutsford and Stockport a token resistance to the royalist advance was provided by Colonels Mainwaring and Dukinfield at the head of the Cheshire militia. After a few sharp skirmishes, they retired to join the Lancashire companies in Manchester, where they awaited the arrival of Meldrum. Meldrum was not there to organise resistance, however, but had merely been sent to Manchester by Fairfax to keep an eye on Rupert's progress, so as to keep those in Yorkshire up to date with the developing situation.

When Rupert arrived on the outskirts of Stockport the defenders had prepared an ambush on the same pattern as that with which Assheton had destroyed Derby's army at Whalley. On either side of the road into the town the hedgerows were lined with musketeers. Rupert, however, was not Derby; he advanced with scouts and outriders in place, and the ambush was detected. The dragoons were ordered to ride down the field side of the hedges, flushing the musketeers from their positions. Once this minor distraction had been dealt with, Rupert, with the main body of the army, was able to advance into Stockport, almost without opposition. In the taking of the town, Rupert made a useful addition to his strength by the capture of a number of cannon with a quantity of ammunition. A more important capture though were the bridges across the Mersey which opened up a route into Lancashire that by-passed Manchester, where the only parliamentary force of any size was located.

The forcing of the bridges at Stockport took place on Saturday, May

25th. As yet the garrison in Lathom House were unaware that their relieving army was already in the county. On the following day, however, they noticed that, when the watches changed, the number of men taking over the new watch seemed much reduced. Their judgement was that morale had finally cracked, and the ranks of the besiegers had been weakened beyond repair. A council of war on Sunday evening decided that with a single, well-delivered push they could probably break the siege themselves. An attack was proposed for first light on Monday morning and captains Ogle and Rawstorne appointed to lead what would probably have been yet another two-pronged attack at the head of two hundred men.

The attack never took place. With first light came the first word from the look-outs, saying that the parliamentary trenches seemed deserted. Soon afterwards Ogle and Rawstorne, cheated of their command, rode out to inspect the siege works and were able to report that there was neither sight nor sound of a single parliamentarian soldier. During the course of the night the whole besieging army had melted away. In the fullness of the morning, the Countess entered her carriage for the first time since the siege began and made a triumphal tour of the deserted siege works.

Rigby received the news of Rupert's imminent arrival on the Sunday and immediately began to make plans to withdraw. It was obvious that the royalist forces would make for Lathom sooner or later and the last thing Rigby wanted was to be caught between the garrison and the relief column. He must have moved some soldiers out right away, if the numbers relieving the day watch were so reduced as to be noticeable to the garrison. The rest moved off under cover of darkness. Initially they withdrew some six miles towards the colonel's headquarters in Preston, halting at Eccleston Green, near Chorley, where Rigby waited for a time in an agony of indecision.

Why Rigby chose to go to Bolton is not certain. According to the diarist it was because he was trying to get out of Prince Rupert's way and thought it wise to keep clear of the Blackburn area. But there are other accounts which suggest that Rigby was sought out by men from Bolton, and was thus responding to their pleas. Personally, I suspect that the account closest to the truth comes from the unknown writer from Kirkham who suggests that Rigby arrived in the town of Bolton almost by accident.

If this version of events is to be believed Rigby was just as over-awed by Rupert's reputation as everyone else, and was very pessimistic about what the immediate future held for Lancashire. From Eccleston, Rigby contacted his base in Preston. This was in a house known as the 'Toye' belonging to Robert Blundell, where two companies of the Amounderness militia were based under captains Pateson and Swarbrick. There were also fifty royalist prisoners guarded by Rigby's marshal, Roland Gaskell. It seems that Rigby was contemplating adding this reserve to the

2,000 men he already had with him because he twice sent orders for the two captains to join him in Eccleston, only to countermand the orders each time. Finally, at some time on Monday the 27th, Rigby's mind was made up. He gave orders for his wife and family to pack up their belongings and retire to Yorkshire until the troubles were over. Then he told his two captains and his marshal that they should take their soldiers and prisoners and go to Colonel Dodding at Lancaster, lodging their prisoners in the castle. Rigby, and the men with him, proposed to march to Manchester, joining the concentration of Lancashire forces gathering there under Meldrum.

If Rigby started out at first light on Tuesday, the 28th, he cannot have got very far, and Bolton was only eight miles away when he heard to his dismay that Prince Rupert and his entire army was between Rigby and his destination, advancing rapidly in their direction. It is very likely that the colonel would have taken evasive action but he was now approached by a delegation from Bolton who pleaded for his help in the defence of the town. Whether he was moved by their pleas or whether he decided that if he were going to have to face Rupert it were better to do so from behind some kind of walls rather than on open ground, it was agreed that Rigby's 2,000 men should enter Bolton and reinforce the 500 clubmen who were the only defenders the town had. Ironically, it is probable that, if Rigby had stayed away, Bolton might have been ignored as unimportant by Rupert – the presence of Alexander Rigby, the 'persecutor' of Lady Derby, far from ensuring its defence, in fact made certain that Bolton would be attacked.

Even amid the burning Protestantism of the East Lancashire towns, Bolton stood out for its puritanical fervour to the extent that it was known as 'the Geneva of Lancashire'. As such it was an obvious target for those of Rupert's forces to whom puritanism was anathema. The town had been fortified and well defended at the start of the conflict, and had successfully defied Derby on two previous occasions. But the fortifications had been neglected and no garrison had been kept in the town since the taking of Warrington in May 1643 had seemed to secure the county for parliament. The Bolton eye-witness account, edited by Ormerod, gives two reasons for this neglect; first, complacency at being so deep in the heart of Protestant Lancashire that they need not fear attack and, second, as a result of disagreements caused by 'woeful and ruin-threatening divisions'.

As a result of this neglect Bolton, prior to Rigby's arrival, had a mere 500 clubmen to defend it, and the only walls were hastily constructed stone barricades thrown across the streets at the entrances to the town. During the morning of Tuesday, May 28th, Rigby added his 2,000 soldiers to this garrison; but they were largely new recruits from the Amounderness militia who had just spent four demoralising weeks in the rain outside Lathom. The Lathom diarist claims that the town was also reinforced by Nicholas Shuttleworth and that the total number of soldiers present was between 4,000 and 5,000. All other reliable sources, however, put the total number at 2,500 if the town's clubmen are included. It was not very many to pit against the increasing strength of Rupert's army.

Assuming that Rigby's 2,000 men entered Bolton in mid-morning after the eight-mile march from Eccleston, they were not given much time to deploy themselves, nor familiarise themselves with their surroundings. Rupert's army was first sighted, a mile to the south east of the town, at two o'clock in the afternoon, so numerous that they looked, in the words of the eye-witness, like clouds or clumps of trees. Estimates of their numbers put them at 12,000, which is probably not an exaggeration given that Rupert had had 10,000 men at Knutsford and had been recruiting ever since. The army spread out and advanced across the Town Moor to the south, small groups of scouts breaking away from the main body to ride up to the barricades to test the defences.

The royalist army displayed its usual indiscipline because a first attack was made before the main strength had deployed itself in battle order. They met with stubborn resistance in a half-hour engagement in which the attack was stopped short at the barricades and then, slowly, was driven back with heavy losses. The royalist front line withdrew to confer and decide their next move. According to Seacome, it was during this pause that a gesture was made by the defenders which inflamed the anger of the royalist ranks. The actual wording reads, 'their captured fellow-soldiers slaughtered on the ramparts.' It could well mean that the garrison executed some of their royalist prisoners in full view of their comrades. If so, it was an act of suicidal folly since Rupert had shown previously that he was ready to exact a terrible revenge on the inhabitants of a town where royalist prisoners had been killed by the garrison. Whether Seacome meant that, or whether the defenders had no more than displayed the bodies of the slain on the barricades, like a gamekeeper lines up dead vermin on his gibbet, Rupert was much angered by their actions and he ordered that in the next attack no quarter was to be given to men taken in arms. He also acceded to Derby's request to be allotted a leading role in that attack since it would be against men whose actions had insulted Lady Charlotte and the House of Derby.

According to the account given by the Lathom diarist, the foot were given the task of leading the next assault but, when some cavalry came out of the town to harass the foot, Derby led a detachment of Rupert's Horse in a bid to drive off the cavalry. This they did, the cornet in charge of the cavalry being killed and a flag captured, which was sent to the Prince as a trophy; just the first of twenty-three colours to be captured that day.

Despite this small success the renewed attack looked to be getting not much further than the first, against extremely strong resistance. And then, according to the eye-witness, the town was betrayed, a local man accepting a large bribe to show the royalists a way into the town through an area known as the 'Private Acres'. After that, as the eye-witness goes on, 'when once the horse was got into the Town there could be no resistance made but every man left to shift for himself'.

In dictating 'no quarter for men taken in arms' Prince Rupert had no doubt intended the rules of war to be followed so that soldiers who laid down their arms before surrendering would be spared, while civilians would not be touched. His men, however, chose to interpret this order to mean that the town was to be given over to the sack. With the cries 'Kill dead, kill dead', 'Where is your puritan God now?' or 'See what your prayers will do for you now', the soldiers rode through the streets, killing indiscriminately and plundering without mercy. Men, women and children were ridden down in the street, dragged from their houses, sabred, pistolled or had their brains dashed out with cudgels. The soldiers died in their hundreds, although some of the raw recruits turned tail and ran; our friend the unknown writer from Kirkham lists over half a dozen officers of the Amounderness militia who were killed there. But it is the civilian deaths which shock most since they were mostly crimes committed for the sake of plunder. The eye-witness tells his own story about how his life was spared by a soldier in return for all the money in his possession, only to be released again so that he was threatened repeatedly, until he got an officer to take him to the Prince for safe-keeping, which the officer would only do after demanding a further twenty shillings as payment for the escort and which the eye-witness had to borrow since all his money had been robbed.

A certain odium attaches to Prince Rupert for the 'Bolton Massacre', although there is nothing unusual in the forces of either side indulging in killing and looting after a place under siege had fallen to the besiegers. What distinguishes the Bolton affair is the extent to which civilians were involved, and the number of cases where prisoners were killed after giving quarter. Having said which, it is not easy to be certain just how many died in Bolton. As always, the numbers of those killed were exaggerated for propaganda purposes. And, again as always, there were many inaccuracies. One parliamentary news sheet lists four puritan ministers whom it says were killed at Bolton, in spite of the names of all four appearing as signatories on a document of 1649. One irony is that the royalist sources, whom one might expect to play down the casualty figures, are the ones with the more inflated figures, and the parliamentarian reports, which might well have propagandised the incident, which give the more realistic numbers. Seacome states bluntly that 2,000 parliamentarians were killed. The Lathom diarist puts the figure at 1,600 killed and 700 taken prisoner. Both these two versions give casualty figures for the parliamentarian side only. A royalist news sheet, on the other hand, gives the figures as 1,200 dead and 600 captured on the parliamentary side, with 300 royalists killed. The eye-witness of Bolton puts the number killed on both sides as 1,200 in all and this seems to be the most credible figure.

In the midst of this carnage one death above all assumed an importance because of the consequences which later flowed from that death. This was the death, possibly at the hands of Lord Derby himself, of a captain with Alexander Rigby's regiment, William Bootle.

The Lathom diarist states that when Derby entered Bolton after the foot had broken through the defences, he met Captain Bootle, who was a former servant of his, and 'did him the honour of too brave a death to die at his Lord's hand.' The implication is that Bootle had somehow betrayed his trust and thereby deserved to die. In this account, however, there is no suggestion other than that Derby killed Bootle in the course of the action to take the town; in fair fight in other words. Other accounts infer that Bootle died after he had surrendered and after he had been given quarter. When Derby was on trial in 1651, the indictment was so framed as to accuse Derby of being 'a man of blood'. Two specific instances cited were, first, Derby's urging Prince Rupert to put Bolton to the sword and, second, that Derby had killed Captain Bootle 'in cold blood'. The Bolton eye-witness calls it a base killing because Bootle had previously been granted quarter, and a number of accounts place Bootle as one of a group of prisoners being held near Bolton Cross when he was seen by Derby who either killed him himself or ordered others to do so. In a variation on this version by Rutter, Bootle pleads for his life with Derby and is told, 'I will not kill you but I cannot save you from others who may'.

In the meantime, another principal actor, Rigby, had escaped from Bolton by the simple expedient of disguising himself as a royalist and riding through and out of town, cheering on the attackers with the cry of 'the town is ours!'

By the time Rigby fled there was no resistance left worth mentioning. Rupert could occupy the town and consolidate his position, taking stock of what he had captured which, apart from the prisoners, included a quantity of gunpowder and match, a couple of small cannon, and twenty-three regimental colours. These last he sent next day to Lady Charlotte at Lathom, sending them under escort by his own personal Lifegaurd commanded by Sir Richard Crane. The captured colours were to hang in the chapel in Lathom House 'as a perpetual memorial' to Rupert's victory and to the gallant stand made by Lady Derby.

Here the diarist ends his account, on the 29th of May, with all the appearance of a 'happy ending' to the first siege. Nothing is allowed to mar that sense of everything now being alright. No word is said to suggest that a second siege followed the first nor that 'perpetual' in this case meant a period of time significantly shorter than perpetuity but more like eighteen months.

Part Three

The aftermath

Chapter Eleven

The march continued – Marston Moor

 UPERT may have relieved Lathom House by his arrival in the county but he showed no immediate sign of wishing to visit the house. Leaving Bolton he turned east towards Bury where, on May 30th, he was joined by George Goring with the cavalry of the king's Northern Army, which had been sent out of York by Lord Newcastle. Goring had been in Leicestershire in the intervening period and he brought with him three regiments of foot recruited in Derbyshire on his way north. When Prince Rupert left Bury, Meldrum, observing events from Manchester, estimated that he had in excess of 7,000 cavalry and 7,000 infantry with him, with more joining every day, attracted by the magnet of Rupert's name.

By now Rupert had half encircled Manchester, from Stockport in the south, through Bolton in the west, to Bury in the north. It is hard to see why, if his aim was to reclaim Lancashire for the king, he did not turn against Manchester at this point, since Manchester was the heart and head of Lancastrian parliamentarianism. Certainly, Manchester was strongly defended. Within the town were the Salford militia, part of the forces of both Lancashire and Cheshire, together with the regiment

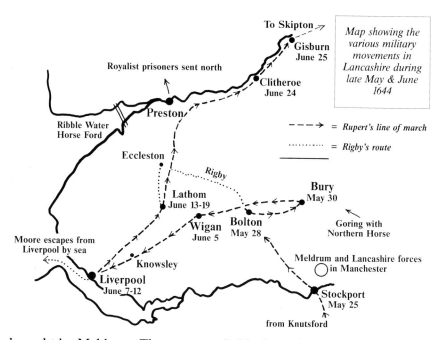

To Skipton

Gisburn
June 25

Royalist prisoners sent north

Clitheroe
June 24

Map showing the
various military
movements in
Lancashire during
late May & June
1644

Preston

Ribble Water
Horse Ford

– – – → = Rupert's line of march

·········· = Rigby's route

Eccleston

Rigby

Bury
May 30

Lathom
June 13-19

Wigan
June 5

Bolton
May 28

Goring with
Northern Horse

Moore escapes from
Liverpool by sea

Knowsley

Meldrum and Lancashire forces
in Manchester

Liverpool
June 7-12

Stockport
May 25

from Knutsford

brought by Meldrum. They were probably fewer in number than those with the prince but they were within walls, and Rupert had sustained enough losses at Bolton not to want to waste his strength on an entrenched Mancunian resistance.

Whatever the Prince's reasoning, Rupert turned west from Bury and headed for Wigan, arriving in the town on June 5th to a very different welcome to that he had received in Bolton. In this strongly royalist town the streets were strewn with flowers on his approach and his name was shouted in appreciation as the deliverer of the town, as if he had saved them from some foreign occupation.

From Wigan he moved on to Liverpool, where he arrived on June 7th. He took his first view of the town from the point on Everton Brow that is still known as Rupert's Hill. At first he was contemptuous of the Castle, which he dismissed as being 'a mere crow's nest which a parcel of boys might take.' Why he should want to take it is not certain. A claim was made that it would provide a suitable port for communication with Ireland, but Chester already fulfilled that role quite adequately and was already in the king's hands. A more likely explanation might well be that he was running short of powder after the engagements near Stockport and at Bolton, and that he lacked arms with which to fit out those recruits flocking to his banner. It was rumoured that there was a formidable arsenal of arms and ammunition in Liverpool Castle and he might well have fixed his hopes on that.

Rupert set up his base on St. George's Plateau where his cannon could easily reach the castle which stood very much where the Victoria Monument stands today. Despite the fact that Moore had a garrison of only four hundred men with which to defend it, the castle proved no easy nut for Rupert to crack. On a promontory between the Mersey and the Pool, the castle was difficult to approach and two attacks similar to the one that took Bolton were repulsed with heavy losses.

The castle held out for five days before the attackers finally got within the defences on June 12th. There followed a rampage of killing every bit as vicious as that of Bolton. This was only halted when Rupert himself entered Liverpool and ordered a halt to it. The victors then turned to plunder but it was soon made clear that their greatest prize had gone. Moore had used the five days' grace lent him by their determined defence to load the entire arsenal of arms and ammunition kept in Liverpool on to ships lying in the river. By the time the royalists broke into the town Moore, with his stock of arms, was away to sea.

It was only after Liverpool was secured and garrisoned that Rupert, with Lord Derby, finally went to Lathom to see his cousin, to receive her thanks and, one would have thought, to congratulate her. But, if the Countess was expecting to receive Rupert's congratulations on her stalwart defence of the house, she was probably disappointed. Rupert might have charmed the ladies and been very chivalrous in his dealings with them but he had very clear seventeenth-century male ideas concerning their role in war and that meant that, in his eyes at least, they should not become involved in military activities.

Rupert's policy at Lathom, therefore, was to get rid of the Countess and to establish the defence of the house on a more professional basis so that it could be left as a secure base in his rear. Lord Derby was told politely that he had done enough and could now return to the task of maintaining royalist government in the Isle of Man, taking his wife and dependents with him. Rawstorne was made governor of the house and given an increased garrison and a perimeter that took in the estate as a whole, rather than just the house itself. Lathom Park and New Park together became a royalist enclave which could dominate Derby Hundred, in co-operation with the newly-garrisoned port at Liverpool.

On Lady Derby's recommendation Captain Chisnall was promoted to the rank of colonel and given command of one of the newly-formed regiments of foot, together with a squadron of horse. From among the experienced officers who had served through the first siege, Farmer was also promoted, being given the rank of major and posted to support Chisnall.

Despite the urgency of the need to relieve York, Rupert seemed to be in no hurry. It was three weeks after he had entered the county before he completed the task of securing the county for the king by taking Liverpool. Now he proceeded to let yet another week go by while he dallied at Lathom. The reason for his doing so seems to have been that he was awaiting the reply to two letters he wrote to the king. What exactly was in these letters we do not know, since they have not survived, and we have to speculate on the basis of what is said in the king's reply. One point made by the king was his inability to supply his nephew with any further supplies or reinforcements, which suggests that a request for these had been the subject of at least one of Rupert's letters. Rupert had expended considerable quantities of powder and shot in the taking of Bolton and Liverpool without, as a result of Moore's actions, being able to replenish them from captured supplies. He had also suffered losses and taken casualties in both of these encounters.

The most significant point of the king's letter comes in what was obviously an answer to a question as to what Rupert should do next. In a very ambiguous statement, Charles says that Rupert should proceed at once to the relief of York but, if that were to prove impossible, then the king would learn to live with it. His actual words were, 'if York be lost I shall esteem my Crown little less'. However, the king went on, if Rupert should decide not to march on York, then the king wanted him back in the south, where the royal army was threatened by a number of difficulties. Rupert had obviously put forward an alternative to a straightforward march on York which the king had rejected.

Rupert received his uncle's letter on June 18th. The next day, over a month after he had set out from Shrewsbury, he finally left Lathom. He lodged in Clitheroe Castle on the 24th, Skipton Castle on the 26th. After spending the night of June 29th in the Fairfax's family home at Denton in Wharfedale, he arrived in Knaresborough on the 30th.

On that same June 30th, the allies withdrew from around York and drew themselves up in battle order across Rupert's line of advance, on Marston Moor to the west of the city. The Prince, however, took a more northerly route and slipped by the opposing armies to enter York on July 1st. York had been relieved.

The battle of Marston Moor was crucial to the fate of Lathom House. It acts like a kind of hinge, linking the first siege, to which it is a suitable conclusion, with the second siege, to which it acts as an ominous prelude. The basic outline of the battle is well enough known. The royalist right, made up of the Lancashire and Cheshire cavalry under Byron, Tyldesley and Molyneux, collapsed before the onset of Cromwell's Eastern Association Horse. The left wing under Goring and Marmaduke Langdale met with much greater success against a hesitant Thomas Fairfax. Chisnall's regiment, fighting in the centre left, made similar good progress, being pulled along by Goring and Langdale. But Cromwell, checking his disciplined men once they had broken the line, wheeled to his right and rolled up the royalist centre and left; his joining with

Fairfax leading to the ultimate victory. Of the contingent sent to Marston Moor from Lathom, Chisnall survived whilst Farmer was killed in action.

The events following Marston Moor are obscure to say the least. A comprehensive survey is virtually impossible because accounts of what the defeated royalist forces did are confused and often contradictory. On the parliamentarian side the only records are often reports of battles and skirmishes which are so confusing that it is frequently difficult to realise that two reports are speaking about the same affair. Rupert's movements after the battle are so apparently aimless as to cause most historians to dismiss them as inexplicable, while rumours in the parliamentarian camp put Rupert in several places at once. What follows is my own attempt to make some sense of what primary evidence is available, set within a framework of what appears to be a logical sequence of events.

We can call Marston Moor decisive because we now know that it was, and that any attempts at a revival of royalist fortunes in the North came to nothing. But we should not ignore the fact that it need not have been so, and those historians who describe Marston Moor in some detail and then immediately switch their attention to the royalist revival in the south-west, following the defeat of Waller on June 29th, completely miss the point that Rupert's apparently aimless and inexplicable wanderings for a month after Marston had as their objective a revival that might well have negated or reversed the results of that battle.

Rupert had fought at Marston Moor with an army totalling 21,000 or more. Even when those killed, wounded or captured are taken into consideration, and even after the defections of men like lords Newcastle and Eythin, Rupert still had a formidable army in the field. This was particularly true of the cavalry. The royalist right had been broken and routed by Cromwell, not annihilated; and the left had been driven from the field, not wiped out. Given time to re-group and recover, they could still represent an effective fighting force.

Immediately after the battle, Rupert returned to York where he re-organised the defence of the city. Two days later, on the 4th, he left the city, heading north with up to 4,000 men, mostly cavalry. When he reached Richmond he was joined by Clavering's horse, who had not been in the battle and who were, therefore, fresh and at full strength. Also in Richmond, on July 6th, Rupert had talks with Montrose, the two men apparently agreeing to a programme of joint action in the Borders near Carlisle.

Rupert then headed back towards Lancashire through Wensleydale and Lonsdale. In the process he detached units and sent back orders to the soldiers remaining near York, so as to make his dispositions according to the strategy that was beginning to emerge. Two castles dominating routes over the Pennines were strengthened: Bolton Castle in Upper Wharfedale and Skipton Castle athwart the Aire Gap. Mayney, with a sizeable force, was set what was thought to be the easy task of raising Lonsdale Hundred north of the sands, the Furness district and the southern flank of the Lakeland hills. Rupert, having established a base in the Kirkby Lonsdale–Hornby area, went on to Garstang where he reinforced Greenhalgh Castle and based Tyledesley in the Fylde and Amounderness. On July 10th, Rupert entered Preston, sending on Byron to be Governor of Liverpool, while Molyneux had a roving commission in Derby and Leyland hundreds. Rupert himself turned back to Kirkby Lonsdale.

In Lonsdale, Rupert was at the centre of what he obviously envisaged as a great Western Counties Association, stretching from the Scottish borders through Cumberland, Westmorland, western Lancashire and Cheshire to Shropshire. The alliance of Goring and Montrose in the Carlisle area would draw off the Scots from around York while a resurgence of royalist strength in Lancashire would threaten Fairfax's flank in the Pennines. On July 30th, Fairfax wrote to parliament with exactly such an assessment, saying that Rupert had only 2,000 men with him but that Mayney in North Lancashire and the Goring–Montrose combination in Carlisle posed serious threats to the parliamentarian position in northern England.

In fact, if Fairfax had but known it, the threat had already passed by the time he wrote his letter. Three factors coming together broke the Prince's vision. First, the Furness adventure, after an initial success, met with a rather more determined resistance than had been expected. Second, the city of York finally surrendered on July 16th, just two weeks to the day after the battle. And, finally, Montrose had become aware of just how he was being used and had withdrawn from the Borders to raise his standard in the Highlands and begin his short but remarkable career.

Rupert left Lonsdale on July 18th, almost as soon as he heard about York. Very quickly he made his way south. On the 21st he arrived in Preston, on the 22nd at Lathom, in Liverpool on the 23rd. By July 25th, he was in Chester, and re-establishing his base along the old Chester-Shrewsbury axis. Even as he left Kirkby Lonsdale, the Northern Horse, quitting Carlisle after Montrose's departure, moved into the Lonsdale area where Goring handed over command to Sir Marmaduke Langdale before hurrying south himself to follow Prince Rupert into Cheshire. The idea of a north-western coalition was not forgotten; merely deprived of the Scottish dimension by Montrose's defection, and with the relief of the siege of York no longer an element in the calculation. Nevertheless, the north and western hundreds of Lancashire remained largely royalist, with strong bases at Greenhalgh, Lathom and Liverpool. If they could consolidate this territory and join up with Rupert in Cheshire, such a grand strategy could still become a reality.

Prince Rupert's reputation might have been dented by his defeat at Marston Moor, but it was still potent enough for it to deter the parliamentarians in Lancashire from taking any action until after his departure from the county. Throughout July and into August they ignored the royalist domination of the western hundreds but consolidated their position in the two eastern hundreds of Blackburn and Salford. As the survivors of Marston Moor returned to their county they naturally based themselves in these two hundreds, gathering their strength.

In Blackburn Hundred the senior parliamentarian officer was Colonel George Dodding of Ulverston, a former deputy lieutenant of the county, sequestrator and Governor of Lancaster Castle. In June he had followed Rupert into Yorkshire, taking with him his own regiment, and also that part of the Amounderness militia that Rigby had sent to Lancaster just before the Bolton affair. Dodding was now re-grouping and re-equipping his forces in the Blackburn area while in close contact with two other colonels, Assheton and Shuttleworth. These forces played a part in the interception of royalist refugees from the battle attempting to return to Lancashire by way of the Aire Gap and the Ribble Valley. It may be noted that Rupert himself, and others returning to Lancashire, did so by the more northerly route of the Yorkshire Dales and Lune Valley.

Following receipt of the letter from Fairfax on July 30th, in which he warned of the build-up of royalist forces in north-western England, Parliament ordered Meldrum in Manchester to take action. It is clear from his actions that Meldrum saw two immediate measures he could take to restrict the royalists' freedom of action. First, he could stop the steady increase in the influence of Lathom as a result of a trickle of refugees constantly arriving at the House; at about the time the second siege of Lathom House was commenced, with a cordon thrown around the house and grounds to act as a sort of ring fence against those wishing to enter. The second action taken by Meldrum was to close the bridges across the Ribble, especially that on the main road at Preston, thus cutting the royalists' lines of communication. Once these two operations had been ordered, Meldrum himself moved. On or about August 10th, he left Manchester with his own regiment augmenting those of the Lancashire forces that were under his command. They were ultimately bound for Preston but, like beaters on a grouse moor, they flushed out pockets of royalist resistance, driving them back.

Ralph Assheton is said to have captured two hundred of Prince Rupert's Horse somewhere in the Preston area, while Meldrum himself is said to have met and defeated three hundred royalists (whom Prince Rupert had left in that county) on their way to fortify Wigan. These reports, and other fragmentary notes concerning skirmishes from the same period, appeared in various parliamentarian tracts at the time, and give the impression that Meldrum and Assheton were jointly sweeping the southern half of the county. On or around the 12th August, Molyneux and the men with him withdrew to join Tyledesley in the Fylde, evading the guard on the Ribble bridges by using the Ribble Water ford between Hesketh Bank and Freckleton.

Parliamentary control of the Ribble crossings was tested on August 15th or 16th, in an action of which we have two versions. The *Discourse of the War in Lancashire* gives the more interesting, although probably the less accurate, version. According to this, 'Now Colonel Nicholas Shuttleworth, lying at Blackburn with his troop upon the 15th of August, he with a part of his troop and some countrymen being desirous to go to Preston if possible (it being the Fair there) when they were come to the Cop at Walton they, meeting with some of the King's party, skirmished with them and put them to flight. And in the pursuit they took a Scots Lord called Ogles and with him one of the Hudlestones of Millom Castle. And after that, they met with more of that company about Ribble Bridge Hill and there had a sore dispute with them . . . they were hard put to that it was with great difficulty that they came off with honour and safety – yet did, and brought their prisoners to Blackburn that night, and went not to Preston'.

This version is interesting if only because it shows that aspects of everyday life such as a fair at Preston could go on in the midst of a war and general confusion. According to the official account 'Lord Ogilvy' and 'Colonel Hudleston' were marching towards Lathom House when they ran into Colonel Dodding and a troop of his soldiers at Ribble Bridge, just south of Preston. There was a bitter struggle in which the parliamentarians came off the worse initially but, falling back on Walton, made contact with Colonel Shuttleworth camped nearby and he came to their assistance. Together Dodding and Shuttleworth counter-attacked, killing many, capturing forty men and fifty horses, and driving the rest to flight. The fugitives tried to reach Lathom House, but were intercepted by the outlying pickets keeping watch on the house. This report speaks of the royalist group being 400 strong and the possibility exists that they were fugitives from this fight who formed either the group encountered by Meldrum near Wigan, or the 200 captured by Assheton near Preston.

The Huddleston mentioned was a member of that numerous family from Millom in Furness. At that time he was presumably serving with Mayney in Furness and it is not certain what he was doing as far south as the Ribble, unless he was carrying despatches from Mayney for the Prince. Such was certainly the intention of the other gentlemen mentioned, as it is certain that the Lord 'Ogles' or 'Ogilby' mentioned is undoubtedly James Ogilvy, 2nd Earl of Airlie, who was an aide to Montrose and whom we know was captured in Lancashire while carrying messages to the king from Montrose. Ogilvy was later sent as prisoner to Edinburgh. The fights around Walton therefore, probably involved royalist couriers with their armed escorts and, although the two accounts speak as if the two actions follow each other closely, there are other versions which separate the two. The fight at Ribble Bridge is accredited to the 15th, with the royalists gaining the upper hand; while that at Walton Cop located on the 16th, with the parliamentarians said to be triumphant. It may well be, of course, that the two men were not together but that the two actions fought were separate encounters with two different couriers.

Whatever the true nature of these two skirmishes, they were to be a prelude to the major conflict of this phase of the war in Lancashire. Late in the evening of August 16th, after a forced march through pouring rain, Meldrum brought his regiment into Preston. On the next day, the Saturday, he was joined by a regiment sent by Sir William Brereton in Cheshire. During Saturday and Sunday he dispersed his forces with the foot billeted on the town of Preston, while the cavalry remained south of the river. It looks as though Dodding and Shuttleworth continued to keep watch on the Ribble bridges, while Meldrum's south-western flank was guarded by Assheton based in the Hoole–Longton area.

On that same Saturday, the 17th, Molyneux and his forces, reunited with Tyldesley in the Fylde, were reinforced by the arrival from the north of Sir Marmaduke Langdale with the Northern Horse. They were a large company. According to the *Discourse,* there were so many that when the head of the column was entering Kirkham the rear-guard was just leaving St. Michaels on Wyre, five miles away. The united army was quartered across three parishes – Kirkham, Poulton and Lytham – with twenty to sixty men billeted on houses big enough to take them. Initially, these newcomers were welcomed as friends by the Fylde royalists but the welcome soon changed when the whole of Sunday was spent in despoiling the countryside of everything they could find. Cattle, sheep, poultry and geese were all slaughtered for food, while any horses to be found were requisitioned as either cavalry-mounts or pack-ponies. The author of the *Discourse* is especially shocked that local people were forced, on a Sunday of all days, to winnow their corn in the open fields to provide fodder for the horses. The manner in which they conducted themselves succeeded in alienating the population in just one day, so that, 'some in the country when they came in said they were their friend that when they went out cursed them, blessing the Roundheads in comparison with them'.

At sunset that Sunday word came of Meldrum's approach. The army decamped from their quarters and made their way to Freckleton at the northern end of the Ribble Water horse ford. By nightfall they were all on the road but were unable to proceed across the ford, as it was too dangerous in the dark. One interesting and slightly disreputable sidelight on the behaviour of the royalist forces is provided by the *Discourse.* In their going to Freckleton, he said, 'they carried along with them many strumpets whom they termed 'Leaguer Ladies'. And these they made use of in places where they lay, in a very uncivil and unbecoming way'.

The army lay around Freckleton all Sunday night, and through Monday morning as well, because there was a high tide and the way across the ford was not passable until early afternoon. It was after one o'clock before they could begin their crossing.

Meldrum on the other hand had ordered his forces to stand to early on Monday morning, the horse to assemble on Penwortham Moor, the foot and carriage in Preston itself. Such were the numbers and confusion that they were not assembled until noon. Then they faced yet another difficulty. It had been Meldrum's intention to take the road close to the northern bank of the Ribble but, with all the recent rain, all the more convenient roads were quagmires and the heavy artillery train was unable to get through. The army had to march north before turning west. The delays were such that, by the time they came to Clifton and were able to see as far as Freckleton, it was to discover that Langdale and his forces were the best part of the way across the Ribble. Meldrum must have cursed the delays in Preston because it was clear that the royalists were making the crossing with the waters still very full. If he had been only an hour earlier Langdale's force would have faced the choice of either having to fight or drowning in an attempt to get away.

In a last attempt to come to grips with the retreating royalists, Meldrum ordered the cavalrymen each to take up a musketeer pillion and to ride as quickly as possible to intercept the fugitives. Despite a desperate ride to Freckleton the pursuers only came within musket-shot of the ford in time to fire on the handful of men who remained as rear guard on the north bank of the river. Meldrum lacked the local knowledge to attempt the crossing where pot-holes and quicksands could so easily trap the ignorant and unwary.

The royalist army got over safely to the south bank but were unable to continue by the direct route because Assheton with his company was blocking the way. They turned instead to follow the southern bank of the river, through Banks, to the parish of North Meols, in what is now Churchtown and part of Southport. There they spent the night and part of the next day. The reason for the delay was probably indecision as to where they should go next. The aim of Langdale, and presumably the others, was to re-establish contact with Rupert in Cheshire without an abandonment of Lancashire. Yet they were not eager to meet Meldrum or a parliamentarian force of any strength. Although there were 2,700 in the party, all but 200 of them cavalry, they were desperately short of ammunition and were reduced to stripping lead from the roof of Halsall Church in order to provide bullets. Wishing to avoid battle and find safe refuge while word was got to Rupert, the decision to head for the safety of Lathom House was made – the House promising not only the security of its walls but also the additional strength of its garrison to swell the royalist numbers and replenish their supplies.

Since Byron came to meet them later, they must have sent word to Liverpool about their plans. Then they left North Meols and proceeded by way of Halsall, and then past Asmall House, by-passing Ormskirk to the south across the face of Ormskirk Town Moor. The probable order of march was Langdale with the Northern Horse in the vanguard, Tyldesley in the centre and Molyneux as rear-guard. The passage round Ormskirk would very likely have been delayed if, as seems likely, the scouts at the head of the column ran into outlying pickets of the force keeping watch on Lathom House. We know that around this time the parliamentary forces who mounted the second siege of Lathom House established their main encampment on Ormskirk Town Moor in the area between Holborn Hill and Prescot Road that is still known as Trenchfields; and Trenchfields lies directly across the path of the royalists' line of advance.

In the meantime Meldrum had returned from the Fylde after having been cheated of his prey at Freckleton, and spent the Monday night in Preston. In the evening he called a council of his principal officers who decided that one positive result of that day's action was that the Fylde was now cleared of royalist forces and it was therefore safe for Colonel Dodding to return to Lancaster, with instructions to attempt to take Greenhalgh Castle en route. Meldrum attempted to get his forces on the march as soon as possible the following morning although, if the confusion of Monday morning was anything to go by, it was probably afternoon before they could set out from Preston. Although the *Discourse* states that he 'marched with what possible speed', he was hindered by his artillery train; it is eighteen miles to Ormskirk, and his men were no doubt tired after the fruitless pursuit of the previous day. It was early evening before Meldrum came in sight of Ormskirk and he can only be regarded as fortunate in that he caught up with the royalists when they were still some way short of their destination and strung out across Ormskirk Moor in no good order.

As far as we can tell the situation with the royalist army was that Langdale had got round Ormskirk and was headed for Lathom, Tyldesley's men were spread out across the moor and Molyneux, in the rear, trailed back along the line of Cottage Lane and Asmall Lane, below the church. Molyneux did not seem to have scouts posted because he was apparently unaware of Meldrum's approach, until a detachment of foot under Booth which had been sent on ahead by Meldrum, fired on the royalist rear.

There then followed one of those unfortunate misunderstandings that were all too common in a civil war, in which like fought like, without distinctive uniforms. At the very moment that Booth's musketeers fired at Molyneux's troop, the relief force from Liverpool under Byron came onto the moor from the south. Completely surprised by the volley that had been fired into their ranks, not knowing where the shots had come from and dazzled by an evening sun low in the southern sky, Molyneux's cavalry mistook Byron's troop for their attackers and turned on them. Some days later Byron wrote to Prince Rupert, informing him as to what had happened: 'They fell in such foul fury upon my regiment that they utterly routed it'.

Booth had virtually nothing to do as Molyneux and Byron destroyed each other, creating total confusion in the rear of the royalist column. Then Meldrum sent in his cavalry and they simply rolled up their opponents and drove them from the field after little more than an hour from when the first shots were fired. It was not an orthodox battle since the royalists were in line of march rather than formed up to receive a charge but then it sometimes seems as if the Lancashire royalists were always to fall foul of a flank attack while on the march. Lord Derby had lost an army to just such an attack at Sabden Brook above Whalley in 1643, and he was to lose yet another at Wigan Lane in 1651. On this occasion they were lost before they began, the line broken before they could turn to meet the attack. Meldrum, 'fell upon them so fiercely that they fled in a most confused manner'.

In Meldrum's own report, quoted in the *Perfect Diurnall* he states 'The 20th of this instant the Lancashire forces near Ormskirk beat the whole strength of the enemy, took about 300 prisoners and 500 horse, killed about one hundred and forced the rest into Cheshire. I have taken Col. Harvey besides seven captains and many other considerable prisoners . . . night-fall prevented further pursuit'.

A newsletter published in *Perfect Occurences* tells much the same story although, being written a little later, it is less confused over the finer details than a report written the same night as the battle: 'On Tuesday in the evening [August 20] our General overtook the enemy near Ormskirk and after some foot of Colonel Booth's had given fire on them they faced about and fled; our Horse bravely following upon them totally routed them. In the pursuit we took 1,000 horse; a list of the chief I have here enclosed. The Lord Byron and the Lord Molyneux were forced to forsake their horse and hide themselves in the corn field'. There then follows a list of prisoners which includes one colonel, one lieutentant-colonel, six captains, six lieutenants, four cornets, two quartermasters, ten gentlemen troopers and two clerks.

Fugitives from the battle fled in all directions. Some no doubt took refuge in Lathom House and probably some of these were to be numbered among the garrison later. Most went for the safety of Liverpool or the horse ford across the Mersey at Hale, these last escaping into Cheshire as Meldrum had said. A few retreated the same way that they came, returning across Ribble Water to the Fylde and further north. A few who had hidden among the corn probably just tried to find the way to their homes, having sickened of the war. Not that they were always successful. Among the list of prisoners included in *Perfect Occurences* is

Lieutenant Thomas Mossock, a local man, from Mossock Hall Farm in Bickerstaffe. He got safely out of the fight and made his way home in the dark, only to be arrested in his own house during the mopping-up operations after the battle.

The Battle of Ormskirk, if it is mentioned at all in the histories of the Civil War, is dismissed as a mere skirmish of no importance, a mere mopping up of isolated groups of royalists wandering through the county in the aftermath of Marston Moor. If for no other reason than the numbers involved, it cannot be so dismissed; at least 2,500 men on each side cannot be thought of as a minor skirmish. Nor is the outcome of the battle insignificant in historical terms. The effective destruction of the royalist army in Lancashire meant the end of any dream Rupert might have cherished of a united North West. It also marks the beginning of the end for Lathom House which, if things had gone differently, might have become the base for Rupert's enterprise. In early August it was still possible to envisage a royalist confederation that stretched from Carlisle to Shrewsbury. By the end of August the only remnants of that dream were the isolated garrisons of Lathom and Liverpool and the last vestiges of Mayney's efforts in Furness. Mayney's venture ended on September 10th, Liverpool finally surrendered in November. Before the end of the year Lancashire had reverted to that situation which had obtained in May before Rupert's arrival, with just Lathom House holding out against a parliamentary control of the county.

It is commonplace to say that the king lost the North at Marston Moor. It could well be equally as true to say that he really lost it on Ormskirk Moor.

Chapter Twelve

The second siege
August 1644 – December 1645

HE second siege has had nowhere near the attention paid to it as was paid to the first. It lacks the glamour of Lady Derby's presence. There was no diarist to chronicle its progress while, in the eyes of a more romantic generation, the wrong side won. Yet in the second siege the garrison held out much longer against much stronger odds in a much less propitious climate, and, in the end, both sides emerged with some honour remaining. It seems unfair that it should always feature as an insignificant postscript when, in fact, the first siege was really no more than a preliminary bout before the main event of the second.

The second siege began after Meldrum received orders to clear Lancashire of the 'malignants'. At first it was hardly a siege, but more in the nature of one armed camp keeping its watchful eye on another; very much as had been the case in the first siege before the intensification of February 1644. It was also much more open, with the garrison far less circumscribed than they had been during the first siege. The garrison was much larger and was not confined to Lathom House itself, but, initially at least, occupied a perimeter that took in the whole of both Lathom Park and New Park, with all the properties that were within them.

At first the watch kept was loose. As had been explained earlier, the original purpose of the siege was less concerned with bringing any pressure to bear on the garrison, than it was with keeping out any new reinforcements who might arrive. The siege lines drawn around Lathom were to keep out, not to keep in. After the events of August 20th, in any case, Lathom ceased to be the focus of attention for the forces of Parliament who by then had become concentrated on the taking of Liverpool, an undertaking that kept them preoccupied until November.

After Liverpool had fallen to Meldrum the Irish who had helped to defend the port, given leave to march to the nearest royalist garrison, chose to go to Lathom, where they formed a good third of the forces at the disposal of Rawstorne, who had been appointed overall commander by Prince Rupert. The cavalry was commanded by Munday and Kay, with the infantry under the control of Charnock, Farrington, Molyneux-Ratcliffe, Nowell and Worrall. Three principal houses were garrisoned – Lathom House itself, obviously, but also a house, known as 'The Lodge' in the despatches of the time, but which, from its description, was obviously New Park House; and also a 'gentleman's house' nearby. The Irish who had been expelled from Liverpool largely garrisoned New Park House.

Even after this strengthening of the garrison in November, Lathom was still largely ignored, even though it was theoretically in a state of siege. Parliamentary policy was changing, with the old-guard, such as Waller, Essex and Manchester, being pensioned off and the regional divisions being abolished. A national army, the New Model, was being formed with Fairfax as its commander and Cromwell as his Lieutenant-General of Horse. With the formation of the New Model Army had come a late recognition of the fact that victory, if it came, would be achieved in the field and not in the taking of isolated, and unimportant, royalist strongholds. They could be dealt with later when the main contest had been settled. Lathom, cut off from the rest of royalist England after the fall of Shrewsbury in February 1645, could be left to its own devices until they were ready to deal with it. Indeed, there is no mention of any action being taken against Lathom between August 1644 and June 1645. Despite the constant presence of parliamentarian forces, who watched their every move, the garrison must have led a quiet if not boring life.

All that ended on June 14th, 1645, when the last major battle of the war was fought at Naseby, where the king's forces were finally and decisively beaten. Charles actually held out until May of the following year, but Naseby had all but ended the war. After June, with the New Model Army making steady progress in re-taking the West, local parliamentarian commanders in all other parts of the country turned their attention to eliminating the remaining pockets of royalist resistance. Between June and the end of the year no fewer than eighteen royalist garrisons were forced to surrender.

Lathom's turn came in the first few days of July when an agreement was reached in Manchester as to the need to reduce Lathom. Many of the same arguments were put forward as had been used by Rigby in the previous year – Lathom was a 'nest of brigands'; they were terrorising the neighbourhood, etc. Despite Ralph Assheton's reservations, the Manchester Committee managed the appearance of unity. The army would be 4,000 strong, drawn from all hundreds of the county, and paid for by the whole county. The overall commander would be Peter Egerton.

We know from Assheton's letter, dated July 2nd, that the siege was well under way by that date, even if Manchester was still arguing over the details. Even so, their first success was quick in coming, when New Park House was taken on the 7th. The light walls were soon reduced by cannon-fire and the house stormed. The report of this action in *Perfect Occurences* claimed that forty of the defenders were killed and sixty taken prisoner. The governor of the house was wounded and captured, whilst twelve officers were listed as either killed or taken. Also among the casualties was a Catholic priest. The same report stated that another house was then under siege by Captain Ashurst, who had taken over those cannon used at New Park, and the capture of that house was expected at any moment. It is not known which this 'gentleman's house' was or when it was that it surrendered, but we do know that by the end of the month all the outer defences had fallen and Lathom House, once more, stood alone.

After the activity of July the period from August onwards resumed a terrible calm, with the besiegers behaving far more circumspectly on this occasion than they had during the first siege. They knew from bitter experience that the house was not open to storm, and nor was it vulnerable to cannon fire, especially with the improved fortifications ordered by Rupert the year before. The besiegers settled into the long process of attrition with their loose cordon around the house based on a main encampment in Ormskirk. This time, however, they could afford to wait because there seemed little chance of any relief coming to the help of the besieged.

In August a Mr John Sharples, Lord Derby's governor of the Isle of Man, together with a Mr Paul, aide to Lord Derby, were arrested by the authorities on their arrival in Lancashire from the island. They were imprisoned for a time and it was suggested that they should be sent to London for trial by parliament. The two men, however, managed to persuade their captors that their sole purpose in coming to the mainland was to carry a message to the Lathom garrison to tell them that Derby did not want them to continue holding out for no good purpose and that they should seek the best terms that they could get. On this basis the two men were permitted to go into the house, partly to communicate the earl's message to the garrison and partly to act as mediators in these first steps towards a negotiated surrender. Whether Sharples and his companion acted in good faith or not we do not know. What we do know is that Sharples reported a garrison adamant in their refusal to surrender. Sharples and Paul were permitted to return to the Isle of Man.

In refusing terms the garrison were pinning their hopes on Charles Stuart, that most unlikely of saviours. Since Naseby the king had been irresolute. He occasionally made forays, but always returned to Raglan Castle, which had become his last stronghold. In early September news reached him of the fall of Bristol to Fairfax, and he dismissed Rupert for having betrayed him. And, having lost one of his two most effective commanders, he naturally thought of the other, and revived a scheme he had proposed before whereby he would combine with Montrose in Scotland. He proposed to march by the western route, relieving Chester as well as Lathom on the way and thus reinforcing his own army before the union with Montrose in the Glasgow area.

Charles left Raglan on September 18th and marched as far as Chester, where he relieved Byron who had been near surrender. From his base in Chester the king sent out the Northern Horse on a mopping-up operation with the object of driving off the last remaining groups of besiegers. However, on Rowton Heath, on September 24th, Langdale ran into Poyntz, with fresh reserves of the Northern Association Cavalry, advancing on Chester from Whitchurch. Penned between Poyntz and the city wall, the Northern Horse under Langdale was denied room for manoeuvre and routed totally. Charles watched their defeat from the city wall before being urged to leave the city, being heard to murmur as he left, 'O Lord, O Lord, what have I done that should cause my people to deal in this way with me?' The king fled first to Denbigh and Newark but found time to send word to Lathom that they should seek the best terms they could as he was no longer in a position to help them.

Despite the collapse of this expedition, the garrison soldiered on through October and into November. Winter was coming on; there was now no hope of a relieving force; and, since there is no doubt that the blockade had been strictly maintained since July, their supplies must have been running low. In late November the garrison asked for negotiations to begin. A location for talks was agreed and three commissioners for each side were appointed. At first all went well. The terms for surrender, as agreed, were that, although the sequestration of his estates would have to stand, a third of them would be returned to Lord Derby. The garrison would be granted the full honours of war and would be allowed to march out of the house in full possession of their colours, arms and personal belongings, with the single exception of the cannon.

It was this last that proved to be the sticking point. Two of the commissioners were ready to accept the terms, but the third refused to sign unless the cannon were included as remaining in the possession of the garrison. The talks broke down without a resolution but, according to the *Discourse,* Rigby informed his fellow officers that he did not believe that the garrison could hold out much longer despite all their bravado. Look at their clothes and the condition of them, he said, and did you notice how they stank, through bad food and shortage of water?

It is the smell of defeat, he said. It was an opinion confirmed very shortly afterwards when an Irish deserter swam the moat. When he was questioned he described something of the true state of affairs in the house. According to him the garrison was short of everything, without hope and beginning to despair. Having heard his account, the besiegers immediately withdrew their offered terms and demanded an unconditional surrender.

On December 2nd the garrison finally bowed to the inevitable and prepared to surrender the house. Rawstorne was totally opposed to any talk of surrender and wanted the garrison to follow him in a last desperate bid and to fight their way out through the besiegers. It was a ludicrous plan because, apart from the overwhelming numbers opposing them, there was nowhere for the garrison to go. Even if they were to have fought their way free they would have found themselves an ill-armed and isolated group deep in hostile territory and surrounded by a county united against them. No wonder that Rawstorne was faced with a mutiny and forced to give way.

The final terms which were agreed granted Rawstorne the rights to his horse, arms and ten pounds in cash. The rest of the garrison were denied either arms or money but were free to go to the nearest royalist towns or garrisons – although, by this time, the nearest such was Ashby-de-la-Zouche. If they wished they could return to their homes without fear of sequestration.

And so, thirty months after Holland's first demand, the house finally passed into the hands of Parliament, and the soldiers who had laboured for so long had their reward at last, as the house was given over to plunder. The gates were torn down and the walls were toppled into the moat. Once the more portable plunder had been removed, the men began to tear at the very fabric of the house in order to sell it for profit. There was an account kept in Ormskirk Church which showed that something in excess of ninety pounds was realised from timber taken from the house. Even more profitable was the lead stripped in great quantities from the roofs of the various towers and buildings. The writer of the *Discourse* feels a sense of disgust at the hypocrisy of the people of Wigan who, while professing to be ardent royalists, were nevertheless to the forefront in profiteering from what they could rob from the house.

It is that same writer, parliamentarian though he may have been, who wrote what must be the most touching epitaph for the house:

Much of that famous house (like a little town in itself) was pulled down and cast into the moat so that it is nothing in comparison to what it was. It was the Glory of the County. The Earls, Lords thereof, were esteemed by most about them with little less respect than kings. It was the headstrong will of the Countess that brought this downfall upon it and when it will be repaired again is doubtful.

It never was repaired.

Chapter Fourteen

Epilogue

URING the first half of 1646 the war dragged on, with the options open to the king gradually reduced. In May, Charles finally surrendered to the Scots at Newark. In January 1647, when Charles refused to take an oath to uphold the Covenant, he was handed over to parliament, but was later siezed by the army. In November, of that same year, Charles rejected the proposals of parliament and once more entered into negotiations with the Scots, accepting the Covenant, and agreeing to impose presbyterianism on England. In return the Scots intervened on behalf of the king and the second civil war followed. Locally there were uprisings in Wales, Kent and Essex that were quickly, and bloodily, put down but the main thrust was a Scottish invasion of England, in August 1648. The Scots were treated with suspicion by the English, and very few English royalists came out in their support. The invading army was effectively crushed by Cromwell at Preston, and finally eradicated in a Scottish last stand at Winwick near Warrington. Parliament, under pressure from the army, proceeded to try and execute the king.

In 1651 Charles II, like his father before him, swore allegiance to the Covenant and was rewarded by being crowned King of Scots. With the young king at their head the Scots invaded England, and got as far as Worcester before being defeated by Cromwell outside that city. The king escaped to France after his famous wanderings and the third civil war was over. The republican Commonwealth followed, to be succeeded by Cromwell's Protectorate after 1653. After Oliver Cromwell's death no worthy successor was found and the country lurched from crisis to crisis until General Monck intervened from Scotland and paved the way for the Restoration of Charles II in 1660.

Many of the people involved in the siege of Lathom House were also participants in some of these events. Lord and Lady Derby retired to the Isle of Man around the time of Rupert's departure for York in June 1644. With them went their children and some of their dependants, including

Rutter. Lord Derby took no further part in the war; nor did he intervene in the second civil war. His one close associate who did so was Sir Thomas Tyldesley who, having spent the last year of the first war as the governor of Lichfield, was to come out again in 1648, and was on the point of capturing Lancaster Castle when he heard of Hamilton's defeat at Preston. Falling back to a defensive rearguard position in Westmorland, he finally surrendered to Ralph Assheton at Appleby in October 1648. After that he retired to join his friend James Stanley in the Isle of Man.

In 1651 both Derby and Tyldesley returned to the mainland to take part in the march on Worcester. Landing near Fleetwood they raised a regiment on Tyldesley's home ground of the Fylde, and set out to catch up with the advancing Scots. Entering Wigan along Wigan Lane they had the misfortune, or lack of judgement, to fall victim to yet another of the kind of ambush that had destroyed Derby's forces at Whalley. This time it was Lilburne who lined the hedges with his musketeers and thus was able to rout the royalists with enfilading fire. Thomas Tyldesley was killed, on the spot where his monument now stands. Derby himself took refuge in an inn and later carried on, virtually alone, to catch up with the Scots. He saw action at Worcester and accompanied the king on the first stage of his escape after the battle. After leaving the king, Lord Derby attempted to make his way north en route for the Isle of Man. But he was apprehended and put on trial in Chester, accused of the murder of Captain Bootle at the taking of Bolton. Convicted, the earl was executed in Bolton, on a scaffold partially built of timbers taken from Lathom House.

After Derby's execution Lady Derby was forced to accept a parliamentary demand for the surrender of the Isle of Man. After a while she left the island to live at Knowsley under virtual house arrest. At the Restoration she moved to London to leave the remaining estate free for her son who had assumed the duties of the earldom. Despite all she had endured in the king's cause she received little or no restitution from the new king and her latter years were not happy. She died in 1664.

Two of Lady Derby's chaplains from the time of the first siege did achieve bishoprics. Brideoak became Bishop of Chichester while Samuel Rutter, who had shared the Derby's exile in the Isle of Man, became the Bishop of Sodor and Man, at the gift of Lady Derby, in 1660. He died in 1663, just a year before his benefactress. Another royalist personality who followed a chequered career after the defeat of the king and who never received the rewards he might have expected on the Restoration, was Marmaduke Langdale. After commanding the cavalry at Ribbleton Moor in 1648, he sought refuge overseas, and served as a mercenary for the Venetian Republic in the Siege of Candia. He returned to England at the Restoration and was at Charles II's coronation, but he also did not receive any compensation and his latter years were penurious.

Lady Derby's principal opponent, Sir Thomas Fairfax, had the most illustrious career of those mentioned in connection with the siege. In February 1645 he was appointed to the command of the 22,000 strong New Model Army, and led that army in the successful conquest of the South West and in the decisive Battle of Naseby. In 1648 he was in charge of putting down the rising in Essex, during which he blotted his otherwise unblemished reputation by the ferocity with which he retook Colchester and summarily executed two of the royalist leaders in the city. Under the Commonwealth he refused to take part in the judical proceedings against the king and grew steadily more disenchanted with the constitutional basis of the republic, under which his position as the military leader was steadily diluted by the greater political skills of Oliver Cromwell. In 1650 he suddenly retired from public life on the grounds of ill-health and spent the next ten years in virtual seclusion at his Yorkshire home.

Of the other parliamentary leaders, Meldrum had died at the siege of Scarborough Castle in 1645. Assheton commanded the Lancashire Foot at Ribbleton in 1648, and then went on to put down royalist risings in Westmorland, culminating in Tyldesley's surrender in October. He died in 1650. In fact 1650 was an unlucky year for parliamentarian colonels. Apart from Assheton, colonels Dodding, Moore and Alexander Rigby all died in that year, Moore escaping retribution as a regicide in so doing. Rigby died as vigorously as he had lived, succumbing to a gaol fever caught while prison visiting in Chelmsford.

And, finally, to Lathom House itself.

Despite a statement to that effect in one chronicle, the house was not reduced 'as if it had never been' by the plunder of 1645. Some part at least remained for the new Lord Derby to live in it for a time after 1660. But, with the walls thrown down and all the lead stripped from the roof, it was little more than a ruin. Lord Derby received no assistance from Charles II and only part of the sequestered lands was restored, so that money was not forthcoming for the repair and reconstruction of the Lathom properties. When the direct line died out and a collateral branch of the family took over, the Stanleys finally gave up Lathom. The Lathom estate was sold to Thomas Bootle of Melling in 1724, and he set about demolishing whatever remained of the old house so as to build a new palladian mansion, designed by Giacomo Leoni, and completed in 1734.

As Earls of Lathom, the Wilbraham-Bootle family transferred their affections to the refurbished Blythe Hall nearby and the second Lathom House declined in its turn. It served as a remount base for the army during the First World War but was largely demolished when the estates were sold off in 1920. Just one wing, in semi-ruinous condition, still stands.

Bibliography and note on sources

IT would be impossible to list all the books I have consulted in the course of researching this book. Some of them contributed no more than an occasional quotation and are no more than peripheral. Others merely repeat, in a simplified form, what is given in more detail elsewhere. I have, therefore, restricted my list to those works which make a positive contribution to this study and which, if all were consulted, should enable the reader to replicate my account.

Primary sources

There are three contemporary, or near-contemporary, accounts of the first siege. The first of these to be published was: J. Seacome, *The History of the House of Stanley, to the death of the late earl in 1776,* published by E. Sergeant in Preston, 1793. This is not the easiest of books to obtain, but the Lancashire Library Service has facsimile editions available for reference. The account of the first siege is supposedly taken from Samuel Rutter's *Memorial of the ever-memorable Siege of Lathom, the defense whereof he had a large share in.* If it was indeed by Rutter it must have been written at a much later date, perhaps explaining why it is defective, with many episodes condensed or omitted and it is quite overwhelmingly biased in favour of Lady Derby.

The second account, and the most important, was *A Journal of the Siege of Lathom House,* originally published by Harding, Mavor & Lepard, London, 1823 (from an original manuscript in the Harleian Library – MSS 2074). Another version of this manuscript is in the Ashmolean, the copy being annotated, in the same hand, 'wherein I was wounded – Edward Halsall'. This last fact has led modern opinion to the view that Halsall was the author of the journal. Previously, it had been ascribed to Chisnall, although Bishop Brideoake has also been mentioned. I believe that the journal contains too much knowledge of Lady Derby's secret counsels and too many classical or other academic allusions to match what might be expected of the seventeen-year-old junior officer that Halsall was at the time. Although I had the pleasure of working with the 1823 edition of the journal, it is a rare book in that form. Again, however, the Lancashire Library Service has photocopied facsimiles of the original edition.

A more practical way of consulting the journal is to use *Tracts relating to military proceedings in Lancashire during the great Civil War,* edited by G. Ormerod and published by the Chetham Society 1844. Ormerod's is a most useful work in that it is composed entirely of extracts from contemporary documents, including not only the journal, but also eye-witness accounts of the Bolton Massacre, John Rosworm's memorial, letters to parliament from Meldrum and others, and so on.

The third account, and the only one written from the parliamentary standpoint, is *A Discourse of the Warre in Lancashire,* ed. W. Beaumont, published by the Chetham Society, 1864. The author is anonymous and I have permitted him to remain so in these pages but all the evidence points to it having been Edward Robinson, a justice of the peace who served as a parliamentary commissioner at the siege of Hornby Castle. This writer is often wildly inaccurate in his dates and chronology, but most of his facts are confirmed by the other sources, and he is extremely accurate in things about which he has any personal knowledge. His description of the bombardment of Lathom House is so detailed that he must have been one of the observers invited by Rigby.

The letter by Ralph Assheton quoted at length in Chapter Eight is one of three letters from Assheton to Norris re-printed in Whitaker's *History of Whalley* (vol. 2, Routledge, Manchester 1872). Other original material can be found in *The Papers of James Stanley, 7th Earl of Derby* vols. 1–3, edited by F. R. Davies and published by the Chetham Society between 1865 and 1867.

Secondary sources

The way in which the siege caught the popular imagination following the publication of *The Siege Journal* can be traced in the numbers of books inspired by the incident which appeared during the last century. A number of these were fictional works, the most famous being Harrison Ainsworth's *The Leaguer of Lathom.* Time has not dealt with these kindly. All nineteenth-century works, whether fiction or non-fiction, tend to be biased towards the royalist cause, while their view of Lady Derby ranges from the sycophantic to hagiography. Two of the more interesting and useful works of non-fiction – albeit somewhat over-deferential – are: Mme. Guizot de Witt, *The Lady of Lathom,* Smith Elder & Co. London 1869; and Peter Draper, *A History of the House of Stanley,* Ormskirk Advertiser, 1854.

Among the histories of Lancashire which feature the history of the Lathom siege there is, of course, Baines' massive *History* and the official *Victoria County History,* although the latter does blot its copybook with careless mistakes, such as its claim that Derby raised 20,000 men from the Ormskirk area. *The Great Civil War in Lancashire* by E. Broxap (Manchester University Press 1905) contents itself for the most part with paraphrasing sources such as the *Journal* and the *Discourse*, often uncritically, so that errors are unchecked. The book is interesting, however, as the first to my knowledge to challenge the location of Lathom House, the author believing it to be situated in the Tawd Valley. More recently, the doyen of Lancastrian historians has been J. J. Bagley. His *History of Lancashire;* was first published by Dorwas Finlayson in the 1950s. A more recent work is *The Earls of Derby 1485-1985,* Sidgwick & Jackson 1985. They are both competent and accurate histories though very much pro-Stanley.

Much useful information can be found in the *Transactions of the Historical Society of Lancashire & Cheshire.* Among the items of particular interest are Arthur J. Hawkes, *Wigan's part in the Civil Wars, 1639-51,* vol. 47, pp 84–138; Steane & Kelsall, *The Park, Moat & House at New Park, Lathom nr. Ormskirk,* vol. 114, pp 73–98; and J. J. Bagley, *Kenyon v Rigby,* vol. 106, pp 35–36.

General histories

For me the best general books about the civil wars are the pair of volumes by C. V. Wedgwood, *The King's Peace* and *The King's War,* Collins.

Most histories of the civil war tend to ignore the war in the North (with the exception of Marston Moor) but two recent books which give the northern viewpoint quite adequately are Peter Newman, *The Battle of Marston Moor,* published by Anthony Bird in 1981; and John Kenyon, *The Civil Wars of England,* Weidenfield & Nicholson, 1988.

Also of interest is a photostat monograph by an adherent of the Sealed Knot Society: Mike Lawson, *For God and the North,* Partizan Press, Leigh-on-Sea, 1984.
